Reviewed
2008-US

PRINCIPLES OF
Islam

Presented to

_____

_____

From

_____

_____

DATE

Also by Maulana Wahiduddin Khan

The Moral Vision
Islam As It Is
Religion and Science
A Treasury of the Qur'an
Woman in Islamic Shari'ah
Islam: Creator of the Modern Age
Words of the Prophet Muhammad
Islam: The Voice of Human Nature
An Islamic Treasury of Virtues
Woman Between Islam and Western Society
Islam and the Modern Man
Muhammad: A Prophet for All Humanity
Muhammad: The Ideal Character
Islam and Peace
Principles of Islam
The Call of the Qur'an
The Qur'an: An Abiding Wonder
The Quran For All Humanity
The Good Life
The Way to Find God
The Teachings of Islam
The Garden of Paradise
The Fire of Hell
Indian Muslims
Tabligh Movement
Man Know Thyself
Polygamy and Islam
Hijab in Islam
Concerning Divorce
Uniform Civil-Code
Introducing Islam
God Arises

PRINCIPLES OF
Islam

Maulana Wahiduddin Khan

Goodword
B·O·O·K·S

First published 1998
© Goodword Books 2001
Reprinted 1999, 2001

Goodword Books
1, Nizamuddin West Market
New Delhi 110 013
Tel. 435 5454, 435 6666, 435 1128
Fax 435 7333, 435 7980
E-mail: skhan@vsnl.com
www.goodwordbooks.com

Printed in India

Contents

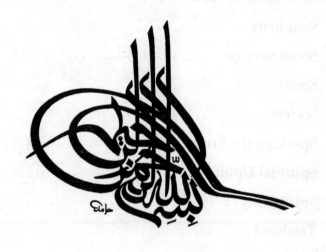

Akhirat

Man is an eternal creature. However, his life-span has been divided by God into two parts. A very tiny part of it has been placed in this world, while all of the remainder has been placed in the Hereafter. The present world is the world of action, while the world of the Hereafter is the place for reaping the harvest of actions. The present world is imperfect, but the world of the Hereafter is perfect in every respect. The Hereafter is a limitless world where all things have been provided in their ideal state.

God has placed His heaven — full of all kinds of blessings — in that world of the Hereafter. Those who prove to be God-fearing and pious in this world will enter into that world to find the gates of heaven eternally open for them.

But those who are oblivious of God in this present world or who opt for the path of contumacy in regard to God's matters, are criminals in God's eyes. All such people will be deprived of the blessings of the Hereafter.

God is invisible in this present world, and will appear in all His power and majesty only in the world of the Hereafter. Then all human beings will bow low before Him. But at that time, surrendering will be of no avail. Self-abnegation and acceptance of God is desired only while God is still invisible. Surrendering before God after seeing Him in the Hereafter will not benefit anyone.

Death is not the end of a person's life. It is only the beginning of the next stage of life. Death is that interim stage when man leaves this temporary world of today for the eternal world of tomorrow. He goes out of the temporary accommodation of the world to enter the eternal resting place of the Hereafter. The coming of this stage in the Hereafter is the greatest certainty in one's life. No one can save himself from this fate in the Hereafter.

Angels

Of the many beings created by God, the angels are of special importance. They have been invested by God with the supernatural power to keep order in the functioning of the universe. They do not, however, deviate in the slightest from the path of God, for all their functioning is in complete obedience to His will.

Diverse and numerous events are taking place at every moment in the universe, for instance, the movement of the stars, the shining of the sun and moon, the falling of the rain, the alternation of the seasons, and so on. All of these, and many other continually recurring events are attended to by the angels. Working in the universe as extremely faithful and obedient servants of God, they ensure the continued existence of the human and animal species on earth.

As well as running the world's systems, these angels,

a numerous band, take charge of all matters in heaven and hell.

The role of the angels can be understood by the example of a large factory. In any such factory, there are many big and complex machines which produce the goods for which the factory has been established. But these machines do not run on their own. To facilitate their smooth running many human hands are required. Therefore, in every factory there are always a number of people whose duty it is to attend constantly to their proper and efficient functioning. Similarly, countless angels are appointed to ensure the proper functioning of the great factory of the universe.

The difference between the two factories is only that in the material one, the human hands are visible, while in the metaphorical one—the great mechanism of the universe—the angels remain invisible to the naked eye.

Man may not be able to see the angels, but the angels can certainly see man, and keep a watch on him on behalf of God. It is these very angels who take man's soul away after death.

Avoidance

Avoidance of friction is one of the most important principles of Islam. Such avoidance means refraining from retaliation on all occasions of complaint and dissension.

By temperament, all men and women differ from one another in many ways. Everyone has experienced the disagreeable situations, arising from such differences. In social life, be it inside or outside the home, it is but natural that unpleasantness should occur from time to time. This is unavoidable.

Now whenever any negative situation arises one way of dealing with it is a head-on clash, i.e. an attempt to solve the problem by direct confrontation. Such attempts are abortive as they only aggravate the problem. In no way will they improve matters.

Islam tells us that on such occasions we should adopt the policy of avoidance. That is, instead of behaving violently and fighting, we should opt for the course of tolerance and forbearance; instead of combating violence with violence, we should adopt the policy of avoidance; remaining united in spite of differences.

According to Islam, it is not only a point of social behaviour but an act meriting great reward. Living with people, and observing their principles are acts which would deserve a reward in normal circumstances, but when one continues to be well-behaved in spite of differences and grudges, by curbing negative sentiments, then the reward is increased manifold. Those who sedulously avoid friction will be counted by God among the possessors of a superior character.

For the human character to retain its superiority there must be staunch and unceasing adherence to the principle of avoidance.

Calling God

*D*ua (prayer) means a call. That is a servant of God invokes his Creator to express either his needs or his servitude to Him. This call in itself is a form of worship.

God is a living and permanent existence. He hears and sees and has the power to do as He desires and set the course of events in consonance with His will.

It is this firm conviction which gives rise to this urge within man to pray to God. When man receives inspiration from God, it comes to him naturally to call upon God for all his needs and to ask for God's blessings in this world as well as in the Hereafter. God is truly man's sustainer.

There is no time set for prayer, neither is there any prescribed method nor a separate language. Man, at any moment, in any form, and in any language can pray to God. If the prayer has come right from inside one's heart, it will certainly reach God. God will hear the call without delay and will answer the suppliant's prayers.

There are certain prayers which are repeated in different forms of worship. But most prayers are not linked to one form of worship or another. For instance, when a man goes to sleep at night some words of prayer come to his lips according to the time. Similarly, when he wakes up, he starts praying to God to help him to make a better start to the coming day. In the same way when he meets someone, or eats and drinks, or takes his seat in a conveyance or is travelling, or is engaged in his economic activities—whatever the occasion—such prayers come to his lips as mean, O God, in this matter you will decide what is best for us.

Dua means seeking from God and this seeking from God has no ending. It continues always. Dua is an expression of unceasing feelings welling up inside the believer's heart for his Lord. No moment of a believer's life can be bereft of it.

∞5∞

Dhikr
(Remembrance of God)

Dhikr, meaning remembrance, that is, remembrance of God, is one of the basic teachings of Islam. The opposite state, that of forgetfulness of God, is unpardonable negligence.

Dhikr is a reality of nature. At every moment man experiences those things which are directly related with God. He sees the sun, the moon, the rivers, the mountains, the air and the water. All of these are God's creations. It is but natural that all the creations that come before man should be reminders of the Creator. Right from the earth to the heavens, all things are manifestation of God's Beauty and Perfection. With their whole existence they serve as harbingers of God's Being.

- Similarly in the world, as man leads his life, day and night, his attention is drawn at all times to God. Being influenced by God's creation, his heart and mind produce divine feelings. *Dhikr* is nothing but the verbal expression of these feelings.

Throughout his life man experiences his attachment to God again and again, and when he ponders over his existence, his heart is filled with rejoicing that God created him in the most noble image and lavished upon him all the best qualities. These feelings well up in his heart in many ways. This is also a form of dhikr.

Man undergoes many kinds of ups and downs in his daily life; he has pleasant as well as unpleasant experiences of all kinds. As he goes through these experiences he repeatedly turns to God and remembers Him in different words, again and again.

Similarly, during his daily obeisance he repeats many prayers. These words of prayer are derived sometimes from the Qur'an and sometimes from the hadith. These words coming spontaneously to his lips are the stuff of *dhikr*, the remembrance of God.

Divine Way

There are countless stars and asteroids in the universe. All of these are incessantly rotating in the vastness of space. Space is like a limitless runway for the movement at great speed of these countless orbiting bodies. But what is most amazing is that neither the planets nor the stars ever collide in their course.

What is the secret? The secret lies in their rotation within their own orbits with the utmost precision and without the slightest deviation. It is this law of motion which has prevented the heavenly bodies from colliding.

Exactly the same course is desirable for human beings. For the human course too God has set a fixed sphere within the limits of which every human being has to move. If everyone moves in his respective sphere, a state of peace is automatically established in society. But when people cross their limits, and break the barriers set for them, society will witness clashes and confrontations. Those who deliberately or even unthinkingly collide with other people will not only invite their own destruction but will also destroy others.

How must man live in social life? How should he deal with others? What should be his behaviour? What norms should he follow in his sayings and deeds? For all this God has given clear commands. He has explained what man should do and what he should not do. In life's daily affairs opting for the course permitted by God is like the stars moving in the orbits fixed for them. On the other hand, indulgence in forbidden things is like deviation from the fixed sphere. It is people who deviate in this way who cause all kinds of evil and corruption, and who, in their straying, destroy not only themselves but also the society in which they live.

The true believer is one who leads his life in the sphere appointed for him by God. It is those who unswervingly pursue the course set for them by their Creator, will share God's blessings in this world as well as His eternal blessings in the Hereafter.

Education

The field of education, covering ethics, religion, skills and general knowledge, is a very broad and very vital one. The importance of learning in enabling the individual to put his potentials to optimal use is self-evident. Without education, the training of the human minds is incomplete. No individual is a human being in the proper sense until he has been educated.

Education makes man a right thinker and a correct decision-maker. It achieves this by bringing him knowledge from the external world, teaching him to reason, and acquainting him with past history, so that he may be a better judge of the present. Without education, man, as it were, is shut up in a windowless room. With education, he finds himself in a room with all its windows open to the outside world.

This is why Islam attaches such great importance to knowledge and education. The Qur'an, it should be noted repeatedly askes us to observe the earth and heavens. This instils in man the desire to learn natural science. When the Qur'an began to be revealed, the first word of its first verse was *'Iqra!'* that is, 'Read.' Education is thus the starting point of every successful human activity.

All the books of hadith have a chapter on knowledge (*ilm*). In Sahih Bukhari, there is a chapter entitled, "The virtue of one who acquires *ilm* (learning) and imparts it to others." In the hadith, the scholar is accorded great respect. According to one tradition, the ink of a scholar's pen is more precious than the blood of a martyr, the reason being that while a martyr is engaged in the task of defence, an *alim* (scholar) builds individuals and nations along positive lines. In this way, he bestows upon the world a real life treasure.

The very great importance attached to learning in Islam is illustrated by an event in the life of the Prophet. At the battle of Badr, in which the Prophet was victorious, seventy of his enemies were taken prisoner. Now these captives were all literate people. So, in order to benefit from their erudition, the Prophet declared that if each prisoner taught ten Medinan children how to read and write, that would serve as his ransom and he would be set free. This was the first school in the history of Islam, established by the Prophet himself. It was of no matter to him that all its teachers were non-Muslims, all were prisoners of war, and all were likely to create problems again for Islam and Muslims once they were released This Sunnah of the Prophet showed that whatever the risk involved, education was paramount.

Islam not only stresses the importance of learning, but demonstrates how all the factors necessary to progress in learning have been provided by God. An especially vital factor is the freedom to conduct research. Such freedom was encouraged right from the beginning, as is illustrated by an incident which took place after the Prophet had migrated from Mecca to Medina. There he saw some people atop the date palms pollinating them. Since dates were not grown in Mecca the Prophet had to ask what these people were doing to the trees. He threreupon forbade them to do this, and the following year date crop was very poor as compared to previous year. When the Prophet asked the reason, he was told that the yield depended on pollination. He then told the date-growers to resume this practice, admitting that they knew more about "worldly matters" than he did.

In this way, the Prophet separated practical matters from religion, thus paving the way for the free conduct of research throughout the world of nature and the adoption of conclusions based thereon. This great emphasis placed on exact knowledge resulted in the awakening of a great desire for learning among the Muslims of the first phase. This process began in Mecca, then reached Medina and Damascus, later centering on Baghdad. Ultimately it entered Spain. Spain flourished, with extraordinary progress made in various academic and scientific disciplines. This flood of scientific progress then entered Europe, ultimately ushering in the modern, scientific age.

8

Faith

The essence of faith is *ma'arifah*, (realization or discovery of God). When a man consciously seeks out and finds God, and thereby has access to divine realities, that is what constitutes faith.

This discovery is no simple matter. God is the Creator and Owner of all things. He will award or punish all, according to their deeds; none is free from his grip. The discovery of such a God shakes to the core of the whole life of man. His thinking is revolutionized, for God becomes the centre of all His emotions.

With God as the principal focus of his attention, man becomes God's servant in the fullest sense of the word. He becomes a man whose living and dying is all for God.

Such a faith ultimately results in all of man's behaviour and his dealings taking on the hue of God. When the believer speaks, he is conscious of the fact that God is listening to him. When he walks, he does so with modesty so that his gait may not be displeasing to God. When he deals with people, he is always worried lest he deal unjustly and be punished by God in the next life.

The impact of this degree of faith makes the entire life of man *akhirat*-oriented. In all matters his eyes are focused on the Hereafter. Instead of immediate gain he makes gain in the next life his goal. Whenever there are two aspects of any matter, one pertaining to this world and the other to the next world, he always prefers the latter.

Faith, another name for the recognition of the Supreme God, becomes for the believer a fountainhead of limitless confidence in his Creator. When this recognition takes root in an individual's heart and soul, his whole personality becomes regenerated. Knowing that in all circumstances he may depend upon God, he becomes a new man.

9

Family Life

The Prophet of Islam once observed: "The best among you is one who is best for his family." This applies to all individuals, be they men or women, young or old. The ideal way for any individual to prove his worth is to become a modest member of his family.

What is a home? A home is a primary unit of social life. A number of homes make a society. When the atmosphere at home is good, the atmosphere in society too will be good. When the atmosphere at home is vitiated, there will be a similar deterioration in the atmosphere of society. Without there being a preponderance of good homes, there can be no society worth the name.

Behaviour at home serves as the first criterion of human goodness. If an individual is very courteous to other members of society, but is rude at home, he will not be considered a good person. This is because it is home life, and not life outside the home which provides the real testing ground for the human personality.

In the ideal home life, elders should show consideration to their juniors, and youngsters should show respect to their elders. Men should treat their womenfolk with kindness, while women, for their part should not create problems for their menfolk. All the members of a family must look to their duties and not to their rights. Everyone should be willing to take his share of the work, but he should also help others to accomplish the tasks allotted to them. Whenever there is any problem at home, everyone should make efforts to nip it in the bud, rather than allow matters to escalate.

The secret of a successful family life lies in willing service and cooperation. Every family member should have the desire to come to the assistance of others and be willing to live in harmony with them, without allowing differences and complaints to mar the domestic atmosphere.

Fasting

*F*asting, a form of divine worship, is observed for one month every year. During this fast man abstains from food and water from sunrise to sunset in obedience to the command of God. This act is performed in order to reduce man's materialism and increase his spirituality, so that he may be able to lead a truly spiritual life in this world. In the process, he spends more time in the worship of God.

Fasting awakens in man the feeling of gratefulness. The temporary deprivation of food and water stresses for him the importance of these things as divine blessings. Then when he partakes of food and water after having experienced hunger and thirst, he can feel how truly precious is the food and water provided to him abundantly by God. This experience increases manifold his feelings of gratitude to God.

Fasting produces moral discipline within man. By

restricting the basic things he desires, the devotee is trained to lead a life of self-restraint and not of permissiveness. What the speed-breaker does for the speeding motorist, fasting does for the devotee.

By having a curb put on his various desires for one month at a time man is trained to lead a life of self-restraint for the whole year, making no attempt to exceed the limits set by God.

What man does by fasting is engage himself more and more in the remembrance and worship of God, and in the recitation of the Qur'an. Thus fasting serves as a strategy to increase the efficacy of worship. In this way God accepts our worship in its heightened form.

Fasting is, in short, a training course. Its purpose is to place man on a special spiritual plane for one month so that he may be better able to lead the life of a true devotee of God and a true lover of humanity.

Freedom of Expression

*I*slam grants human beings total intellectual freedom. Rather it would be truer to say that it was Islam which for the first time in human history brought about a revolution in freedom of thought. In all the ages of history prior to Islam, the system of despotism prevailed, and man was consequently denied freedom of thought. This was a matter of the utmost gravity for it is a fact that the secret of all human progress lies hidden in such freedom.

The first benefit of intellectual freedom is to enable man to achieve that high virtue which in the Qur'an is called "fearing the unseen." That is, without any apparent compulsion or pressure from God, man, of his own free will, acknowledges God and leads his life in this world, going in fear of Him. In the absence of an atmosphere of total freedom, no one can undergo this spiritual experience—an indescribable spiritual pleasure—which is called in the Qur'an, going in fear of the Lord. Without such freedom it is not possible to give credit to anyone for this highest of human virtues.

Man is a thinking creature. Of necessity he forms opinions. If curbs are placed on the independent expression of his views, the content of his thought may remain unchanged, but his ideas will never find expression in his speech and writings. Curbs of this nature, imposed by a community or a state, will ultimately produce a society of hypocrites. No sincere person can ever flourish in such a repressive atmosphere. It is only freedom of thought and expression which can save man from hypocrisy.

Moreover, intellectual freedom is directly related to creativity. A society with freedom of thought will produce creative human beings: a society which places curbs on freedom of expression will necessarily witness intellectual stagnation; it will stop producing creative minds, and its development will come to a standstill.

In matters of criticism or expression of differences, the right approach is for people to end unnecessary sensitivity to it instead of attempting to put an end to criticism and differences. This is the demand of Islam as well as of nature.

According to the hadith it is a virtue on the part of believers: to accept the truth without any reservation when it is presented to them. That is to say, a believer is one who has the ability in the perfect sense of the word to accept the truth. Whenever truth is brought before him, whenever his faults are pointed out to him, no complex comes in the way of his accepting of the truth.

This quality is present to the maximum degree in one who is ready and waiting to accept the truth when it is brought before him. Eager for his own improvement, he accepts the truth with pleasure. This keenness for self-reform through acceptance of the truth is perfectly expressed in the words of 'Umar ibn al-Khattab: "May God bless the man who sends me gifts of my own shortcomings."

It is a fact that acknowledgment of truth is worship, nay, it is the greatest form of worship. It is an act for which man has to make the greatest sacrifice. What makes it such a great sacrifice is that it involves the setting aside of one's prestige.

It amounts to the sacrifice of one's ego. But that is the occasion when man assures his entry into heaven.

When does one find the opportunity for this great form of worship and this great good fortune? This opportunity comes one's way only when there is full freedom of expression. When one can criticise another with impunity. When such an atmosphere prevails in a society which permits the speaker to air his views freely and the listener may freely appreciate what is being said. Just as a mosque is the right place for the performance of prayer in congregation, similarly freedom of expression is the right atmosphere in which to foster the great virtues of expressing the truth and acceptance of the truth.

Fundamentalism

*F*undamentalism literally means to stick to the fundamentals or to stick to the basic teachings of a religion. As religious terminology this term originated in the early period of the 20th century. In its initial stages it was mainly a Christian phenomenon. Modernist Christians attempted to give a liberal interpretation to some biblical teachings like the concept of the virgin birth; atonement and resurrection etc.

The conservative Christians refused to accept this kind of liberal interpretation. They maintained that the Bible was a sacred book and that they were bound to take all its teachings verbally. So the term fundamentalism was applied to the conservatives as against the liberals.

Later this term in its extended meaning began to be applied to other religions also, for instance, Islamic fundamentalism or Muslim fundamentalists.

The same story was repeated here also. Muslim modernists too started to give a liberal interpretation to the traditional teachings of Islam. Again the conservative Muslims opposed such a move. These Muslim conservatives came to be known as fundamentalists.

For instance, according to the traditional concept, the Qur'an was a book of God. The modernist Muslims attempted to give this concept a new interpretation. They said that the Qur'an came into being through divine inspiration received by the Prophet and that this inspiration was expressed by the Prophet in his own words. Thus although the Qur'an is a revelation of God, it is in the words of Muhammad (PBUH). Now the conservatives among the Muslims refused to accept this interpretation. They insisted that the Qur'an was the book of God both in word and meaning. This resulted in a controversy between the two groups of Muslims. One group came to be known as modernists and the other group as fundamentalists.

Nowadays fundamentalism has two meanings. To me one meaning is right, the other meaning is wrong.

One meaning of Islamic fundamentalism is to take it in the sense of sticking to the fundamentals, called *ittiba'*, adhering to them in both letter and spirit.

Present age is the age of religious freedom. If someone says that he will adhere to his religion literally, there is no reason to raise an objection. Such a person is only exercising his religious freedom. But if Islamic fundamentalism is taken in the second meaning of imposing it on others by force, for instance, if some Muslims hold that they will not compromise with others in the matter of their religion, and that they have to impose the teachings of their religion on others by force, then in such a case, Islamic fundamentalism will go against the spirit of Islam as well as reason.

This second concept of Islamic fundamentalism has produced what is known in modern times as Islamic extremism or Islamic terrorism. But the truth is that the terms Islamic extremism or Islamic terrorism are self contradictory. Islam is a religion of tolerance and peace. It is defamatory to attribute the words terrorism or extremism to Islam. In fact, there is no room for terrorism or extremism in Islam. The Prophet of Islam has observed: "The religion revealed to me is a religion of kindness and tolerance." There is no room for violence in Islam for any reason whatsoever. Thus Islamic fundamentalism in this second sense is not acceptable to Islam.

After the second world war, however, some Muslims opted terrorism or extremism in the name of Islam to achieve political ends. It was their personal act. But since they carried it out in the name of Islam it was attributed by the people to Islam. The truth is that this is a misuse of Islam. It has nothing to do with Islam. Those Muslims who are engaged in terrorism or extremism in the name of Islam are certainly misusing Islam.

Islam is a scheme of spiritual development. The goal of Islam is to establish direct communion between God and man in order that man may become the recipient of divine inspiration. In such a religion it is moderation which is of the utmost importance, not extremism. It is peace which is of the utmost importance and not violence. From this we can understand what is and what is not included in Islamic fundamentalism.

Gaining or Losing

*I*n this world man sometimes loses, sometimes gains. These vicissitudes are the common lot. No one is exempt from them.

Now the question is how man should react to them. Islam tells us that both these experiences are meant as tests. Here gaining is not in itself synonymous with success. Similarly, losing does not mean that an individual has failed for all time.

Losing and winning are not in themselves important. What is of actual importance is how people conduct themselves when facing these experiences.

So, when a man suffers a loss, he should not consider himself a failure and a deprived person; he should not lose hope and courage, and begin uttering endless complaints. He must rather prove his courage, and, bearing up under the burden of adversity, retain his mental balance. He must consciously regard both the "give" and the "take" as being from God. He has thus to accept God's decisions. For it is by his willingness to do so that he will entitle himself to a share in God's mercy.

Similarly, when he has the experience of gaining he should not become haughty and start regarding himself as superior to others.

On the contrary, success should only increase his modesty. He should become all the more particular regarding his duties in relation to God and humanity and perform them the more rigorously.

In this world, losing and gaining are both forms of testing. Neither is the loser a failure, nor is the gainer a success. The actual criterion of success and failure is how each has reacted to those situations.

The successful person is one who keeps his balance and composure whether gaining or losing. Neither experience should make him deviate from the path of moderation. Those who remain on this straight and narrow path are successful in the eyes of God. Nothing will hinder their progress towards success.

God

God is One, Eternal and Absolute. He is everything, everything is from Him. God, the Creator of all things is the Sustainer of the universe.

> *Allah: there is no deity save Him, the Living, the Eternal One. Neither slumber nor sleep overtakes Him. His is what the heavens and the earth contain. Who can intercede with Him except by His permission? He knows all about the affairs of men at present and in the future. They can grasp only that part of His knowledge which He wills. His throne is as vast as the heavens and the earth, and the preservation of both does not weary Him. He is the Exalted, the Immense One.*
>
> (2:255)

Say: 'Allah is One, the Eternal God. He begot none, nor was He begotten. None is equal to Him.'

(112: 1-4)

Chapter 112 of the Qur'an, entitled *Ikhlas*, gives us the essence of monotheism. Not only does it tell us of the oneness of God, but it also makes it clear what the oneness of God means. This chapter presents the concept of God, purified of all human interpolation, for, prior to the advent of Islam, tampering with the sacred text had caused this concept of God to be distorted for all would-be believers. God is not many. He is only one. All depend upon him. He depends on none. He, in his own being, is all powerful. He is above to beget or begotten. He is such a unique being who has no equal or compeer. All kind of oneness belongs to this Almighty Being. The concept of One God is the actual beginning point and also the only source of Islamic teachings.

God-Oriented Life

The goal of Islam is to induce man to give up his ungodly ways, so that he may lead a totally God-oriented life. One as yet untouched by Islam directs his attention towards things and beings other than God. That is, he is concerned with creation rather than the Creator. Islam shows him how to focus his thoughts and feelings on God alone. When man adopts a path directed to a certain destination, he considers it necessary to keep to that path without turning to the left or the right. For if he makes constant detours, he will fail to reach his destination. The same is the case with man's journey towards his Maker.

In this world when a person sets out on journey, he finds two paths, one leading to God and the other path to different destinations. Now the way of the true seeker of God is to take extra care to adhere strictly to the path of God, without ever turning off it. One who adheres to the straight path leading towards God will without doubt reach God. On the other hand one who turns off at every bye-lane will be lost on the way. His path will never lead him towards God.

What this deviation means is that he has become subservient to his desires attaching importance to immediate interests; he has fallen prey to negative feelings such as anger, hatred, jealousy, egoism, etc.; or he has simply run in any direction he finds open before him, without giving his destination much thought.

On the other hand, the God-oriented path is one on which he earnestly considers God's commands. He sets his course after serious deliberation, on the basis of accountability, instead of pursuing immediate gains or temporary satisfactions.

God's Blessings

Right from a glass of water to political power, everything that people possess in this world is from God. Everything is a direct blessing of God. Whatever one finds in this world is there because of the will of God. If God does not will it, no one can have anything, no matter how hard he tries for it. This is an undeniable truth proved by the Qur'an and the Hadith.

Another thing that we learn from the Qur'an and the hadith is that there are two forms of divine blessing. One special and the other general. Political power is a special blessing of God. We learn from the Qur'an that political power is not given to everyone. Neither can it be received through political movements or the gun culture. It is directly related with the way of God. One of the *sunnah* of God is that if a group proves, in the real sense of the word, to have true faith and to be virtuous in action, then God grants that group political power:

Allah has promised those of you who believe and do good works to make them masters in the land (24:55).

That is, even when power is desirable, the movement will begin from the point of character building and individual reform instead of political action.

Then God's general gift is what is shared, more or less by everyone. In principle, it consists of two kinds of things—peaceful circumstances and the easy availability of the necessities of life. This we learn from the following verse of the Qur'an:

God has made an example of the city which was once safe and peaceful. Its provisions used to come in abundance from every quarter: but its people denied the favours of Allah. Therefore, He afflicted them with famine and fear as a punishment for what they did. (16:112)

Two things in this verse are called the blessings of God: peace and provision. It shows that from the worldly point of view these two things are essential for human beings. If a group comes to possess these two things, then it should not wage war for anything else, such as political power. Rather considering those blessings to be sufficient, believers should engage themselves in thanksgiving to God, until God himself paves the way for whatever else is to come.

What is thanksgiving to God? It is that whatever God

has given us should be put to proper religious and constructive use. Remaining content with what one already has is thanksgiving, whereas regarding what one already possesses as unimportant and launching stormy movements for things not in our possession is ungratefulness.

Any Muslims in possession of both peace and provision ought to occupy themselves with spiritual matters rather than political activities. Now is the time to engage themselves in producing spiritual fervour in their people; in launching movements of moral reform; in educating their people; in planning the way to communicate God's message to other communities; in spending their time in their places of worship, in developing their academic institutions, in setting up their settlements as a model abode of godly people, etc.

This is true thanksgiving. This is to pay the due of God's blessings. A non-believer's eyes are on his rights while a believer's eyes are on his responsibilities. That is why an unbeliever is always running for what he has yet to possess, while a believer always engages himself in discharging his responsibilities within his own sphere.

Those who do not follow the path of thankfulness, launch heated movements towards political goals or revive the gun culture against their supposed enemies. Such people are undoubtedly anarchists. Their case is one of adding insult to injury, even if their movement has been launched in the name of Islam.

For such people it is the decree of God that they never reach their political goal, and whatever blessings of peace and worldly provision they have already enjoyed be denied to them. They will lose what they already possess. This is the way of God.

17

God's Servant

Man is God's servant. Man has been created by God with a plan, that is, to place him temporarily on earth in order to test him. Then those who pass this test will be rewarded, while those who fail will be rejected.

For the purposes of this test, man has been granted freedom in this world. Whatever man receives in this world is not as a matter of right but only as a matter of trial. Every situation here is a test, and in all situations man must give a proper performance, as is required of him by God.

The proper attitude for man is not to take to the paths of his desires, but to try to understand the divine plan of creation and then after being convinced of its ineluctability, he should build his life accordingly.

Man may deviate from the divine plan by misusing the freedom given to him by God, but he cannot save himself from the consequences of this deviation.

In such a state of affairs, it is in the interest of man himself that he remain extremely cautious in determining the course of his life. Instead of being guided by his own will and desires, he should make God's will his guide. Instead of pursuing his own desires, he should lead a life in conformance with the commands of God.

Man may be a masterpiece of divine creation, but he must nevertheless remain subservient to the plan of God. Making a full acknowledgement of these two aspects of the existence of mankind is the key to human progress.

Man succeeded in building a modern industrial civilization by discovering and exploiting the laws of nature. Similarly in the next world man will achieve lasting success on a much vaster scale, but only after striving earnestly to comprehend the creation plan of God for humanity and then adhering unflinchingly to its edicts.

18

Good Character

Good character is the sum of personal virtues which guarantees correct and agreeable behaviour in daily social interaction. A person of good character will invariably conform in his behaviour to a strict code of ethics.

What should be the underlying principle of this code of ethics? According to a hadith it is simply this—you should like for others what you like for yourself, that is, you should treat others just as you want to be treated by others.

Everyone likes to be addressed with good manners and pleasing words. So everyone should speak gently to others. Everyone wants his existence to be problem-free, so he should avoid creating problems for others.

Everyone wants others to deal with him in a sympathetic and cooperative manner. So what everyone ought to do while dealing with others is to give them his full sympathy and cooperation.

This standard of ethics is very simple and natural. It is so simple that anyone may easily learn it, be he literate or illiterate, able bodied or disabled, and regardless of his likes and dislikes. This hadith has given such a criterion for human ethics that no one can find difficult to understand. In this way Islam has set forth, in the light of everyone's personal experience, what behaviour may be indulged in and what behaviour has to be refrained from.

According to another hadith, the best of us is one who is best in moral character. Accordingly, becoming a good human being has nothing ambiguous about it. Its simple formula is that of avoidance of double standards. One who lives his life by this formula is indubitably a person of the highest moral character.

19

Greater Jihad

Jihad is regularly misconstrued as war, with all its connotations of violence and bloodshed. However, in the Islamic context, and in literal sense, the word *jihad* simply means a struggle—doing one's utmost to further a worthy cause. This is an entirely peaceful struggle, with no overtones even of aggression. The actual Arabic equivalent of war is *qital*, and even this is meant in a defensive sense.

According to Islamic teachings, *jihad* is of two kinds. One is with the self (*jihad bin nafs*), that is, making the maximum effort to keep control over negative feelings in one's self, for instance, arrogance, jealousy, greed, revenge, anger, etc. The psychological efforts to lead such a life of restraint is what *jihad bin nafs* is about. In social life, it happens time and again that all sorts of base, negative feelings well up within a man, causing him to lead his life succumbing to desires and temptations. The internal effort made in such a situation to overcome the temptations of the self and to continue to lead a life guided by principles is the truly Islamic *jihad bin nafs*.

According to the Hadith, a believer is one who wages *jihad* with himself in the path of obedience to God. That is, at moments when the self (*nafs*), lured by some temptation, desires to deviate from the path of God, he keeps control over it and remains unswervingly on the divine path. This is his *jihad*—a permanent feature of the life of a believer, continuing day and night, and ending only with death.

The other form of *jihad* is that which is engaged in to propagate the constructive message of Islam. All those who embark upon such a course must first of all study the Qur'an and sunnah in a dispassionate and objective manner. No kind of conditioning should be allowed to come in the way of such study. Only after passing through this intellectual *jihad* will the would-be proponent of Islam be in a position to make a true representation of his religion.

Two conditions have been laid down in the Qur'an for the communication of the teachings of Islam to others—*naasih*, well-wishing and *amin*, trustworthiness. The former appertains to God and the latter to man.

What is meant by *naasih* (well-wishing) is an earnest desire on the part of the preacher of truth for the well-being not just of his immediate interlocutors, but the whole of humanity. This well-wishing should be so steadfast that it remains undiluted even in the face of injustice and oppression. Overlooking people's negative behaviour towards him, the preacher should continue to remain their well-wisher.

The element of trustworthiness (*amin*) is important in that it ensures that the religion God has sent to the world will be presented to the people without deletion, addition or distortion. For instance, if the Islam sent by God is *akhirah* (Hereafter) oriented, it should not become world oriented; if it is spiritually based, it should not become politics based; if it confines *jihad* to peaceful struggle, it should not become violence based.

Islam asks us to perform *jihad* by means of the Qur'an, calling this 'greater' *jihad* (25:52). But it never asks its believers to do the 'greater' *jihad* by means of the gun.

This is a clear proof that *jihad* is, in actual fact, a wholly peaceful activity, carried out through peaceful methods. It has nothing to do with violent activities or violent threats.

Jihad through the Qur'an means striving to the utmost to present the teachings of the Qur'an before the people. That is, presenting the concept of One God as opposed to the concept of many gods; presenting *akhirah*-oriented life as superior to world-oriented life;

principle-oriented life as against interest-oriented life; a humanitarian-oriented life as more elevated than a self-oriented life and a duty-oriented life as a categorical imperative taking moral precedence over a rights-oriented life.

Jihad, according to Islam, is not something about which there is any mystery. It is simply a natural requirement of daily living. It is vital both as a concept and as a practice because, while leading his life in this world, man is repeatedly confronted by such circumstances as are likely to derail him from the humanitarian path of the highest order.

These factors sometimes appear within man in the form of negative feelings. This is something to which everyone must remain intellectually alert, so that if for any reason there is some danger of a negative mindset gaining the upperhand, he may consciously and deliberately turn himself to positive thinking. Even if circumstances repeatedly place him in situations which are depressing and demoralising, he must never on such occasions lose courage or lose sight of noble goals. The re-assertion of his ethical sense is the real *jihad* which he has to wage.

From the Islamic standpoint, intention is all-important. Any undertaking carried out with good intentions will win God's approval, while anything done with bad intentions is bound to be disapproved of and rejected by God. In actual fact, intentions are the sole criteria of good or bad actions in the divine scheme of things.

This truth relates *jihad* to man's entire life and to all of his activities. Whatever man does in this world, be it at home, or in his professional capacity, in family or in social life, his prime imperative must be to carry it out with good intentions and not the reverse. This, however, is no simple matter. In all one's dealings, adhering strictly to the right path requires a continuous struggle. This is a great and unremitting lifelong struggle. And this is what is called *jihad*.

Even if one is engaged in good works, such as the establishment and running of institutions which cater for social welfare or academic needs, or if one is personally engaged in social work or performing some service in the political field, in all such works the element of personal glory has a way of creeping in. Therefore, in all such instances, it is essential that in the individuals concerned there should be a strong tendency to introspection, so that they may keep before them at all times the goal, not of personal glory but the greater glory of God.

It is one's intense inner struggle to make all activities God-oriented which is truly Islamic *jihad*.

20

Hajj

*H*ajj, pilgrimage, is an act of worship. It is obligatory only for those who are in good health and who can afford to perform it. The indigent and the sick or disabled are excused.

In order to perform Hajj, the individual leaves his home for Hijaz, Mecca and Medina. On entering Mecca he goes to the Kaaba to perform its circumambulation. Then he does a brisk walk (*sa'i*) between the two hillocks Safa and Marwa, halts at Arafat, casts stones at Jimar, then sacrifices an animal. These are the main rites of Hajj performed in the month of Dhul Hijja.

Hajj is a symbolic expression of man's full surrender before his Lord. Through the acts which make up Hajj the servants of God make a covenant of giving themselves entirely up to their Creator. Their lives will revolve around God alone. They are prepared to make any kind of sacrifice for the Almighty.

During the rites and rituals of Hajj, the pilgrims recall the sacrifices made by the architects of the Kaaba—the Prophet Abraham and his son Ishmael. The pilgrims also visit those historical places which relate to the life of the Prophet Muhammad. They spend a few weeks in such surroundings, the scene of early Islamic history.

In this way the Hajj becomes a means of linking the pilgrim to God and his messengers, and reminds him of the upright lives led by the pious servants of God. In effect, it creates the possibilities of live contact with the history of Islam.

Over and above this, Hajj unites worshippers the world over. It refreshes the minds of the believers with the reality that although they belong to different races and nations, the belief in one God serves as a strong basis for universal unity. However diverse in upbringing they may be, and whatever the country or nation to which they belong, in respect of their being worshippers of God, they are all one and will always remain united. Hajj is in essence an act of worship, but in practice it affords many benefits affecting the entire Muslim brotherhood, one of these being national unity.

21

Human Brotherhood

According to Islam, all human beings have been created by one and the same God, and for this reason belong to one great brotherhood. So far as their earthly origin is concerned, they are all descendants of the first pair of human beings ever created by God — Adam and Eve. In their subsequent spread over different parts of the world, variations in geographical conditions produced a diversity of skin colourings, languages and other racial characteristics.

The teaching of Islam in this regard is that despite differences of colour, language, etc., people should harbour no ill-will towards those who are apparently unlike themselves, for differentiating between one man and another is not approved by God. They should rather promote fellow feeling towards others, even if at first glance they appear like total strangers to them. Bearing in mind that they are all traceable back to Adam and

Eve, they should be each other's well-wishers and willingly come to one another's assistance, like members of the same large family.

Ideally, the relation between one man and another ought not to be one of strangeness but one of familiarity; not of distance but of nearness; not of hatred but of love.

When all human beings are descendants of the same progenitors, that means that all are equal: no one is superior or inferior. The distinction between great and small is not between one human being and another, but between God and man. And before God, certainly, all human beings are equal; all are equally His creatures and His servants. For God does not discriminate between one or the other of His creations.

Human Equality

According to Islamic tenets, all human beings are equal. In prayer, all members of the congregation stand in the same rows together, and on the Hajj pilgrimage, all the believers belonging to different countries don identical white seamless robes for the performance of the obligatory rites. On the occasion of the Final Pilgrimage, it is noteworthy that the Prophet of Islam declared that no Arab was superior to a non-Arab and that no white was superior to a black. All were equally servants of God. In Islamic society, everyone is accorded the same status, there being, ideally, no higher or lower social strata.

How then can we rationalise what are apparently very great differences in human beings in terms of colour and race, etc., considering that the concept of human equality ranks so high in the value system of Islam? We find the answer in the Qur'an, which makes it clear that such outward differences are meant to serve as means of identification and were never intended as indicators of superiority (or inferiority). People in different parts of the world may have a diversity of skin colourings and other distinctive racial characteristics, but that is only so that they may be easily distinguished from each other. By Islamic standards, this is designed to facilitate social and national interaction.

The sole basis of superiority in Islam is *taqwa* — the earnestness with which one leads a God-fearing life; as such, it bears no relation to colour or race. Physical attributes certainly have their effect on the social interaction of this world, but in the Hereafter, no value is attached to them. There, the only things which count are inner qualities, for upon them depends the essential excellence of man's distinctive character. That is why, according to a hadith, God sees the heart and not the body. He reserves a place in Paradise only for those found deserving in terms of their inner worth.

According to Islam, all greatness belongs to God. God as the Supreme Being is ineffably superior to all men. While there is this infinitely great difference between God and man, there is no difference whatsoever between man and man.

Intentions

*I*slam attaches the utmost importance to intentions (*niyyah*). No action is acceptable to God purely on the basis of its outer appearance. He accepts only such actions as are performed with proper intention, and rejects those performed with ill-intention. Right intention is the moral purposiveness which underlies all actions performed solely for God's pleasure. One who acts on such feelings will be rewarded by God in the Hereafter.

Ill-intention, on the other hand, is a negative spur to worldly attainment. Ostensibly religious acts, if performed for worldly gain or public commendation, are in this sense ill-intentioned. Any fame, honour or popularity which ensues from an ill-intentioned act is a hollow triumph and is looked upon by the Almighty with extreme disfavour.

Intention is rooted in man's inner thinking and feelings. A common man is unable to penetrate the inner recesses of a person's mind but God knows full well what a man's thought processes and feelings are. People can be deluded by appearances, but God has complete knowledge of everything. He will deal with people according to His knowledge and will reward everyone exactly as he or she deserves.

Intention has to do with the inner reality. A thing which loses its reality or its meaningfulness is valueless. Similarly, an act which is performed with ill intention or with no good intention, has no value—neither in the eyes of man, nor of God.

Things are of value only when they are pure, without any adulteration. An act done with right intention is a pure act, and an act performed without right intention is an impure act.

Jihad

Jihad means struggle. Any sincere effort for the cause of religion will be called Jihad. Man's self leads him to evil. So waging war with the self is jihad. Sometimes friends or acquaintances pressurize you into engaging in activities which are not right from the moral standpoint. At that time, refusing to yield such pressure and sticking firmly to an upright attitude are forms of jihad.

Exhorting people to goodness and making them refrain from indecency are tasks entailing a great struggle. Continuing the dawah campaign whilst bearing all hardship is also jihad.

If having been treated with bitterness by neighbours or acquaintances, or after suffering any other kind of provocation, one refrains from reaction and retaliation and maintains pleasant relations unilaterally, this will also be a form of jihad.

There is another kind of jihad which is called 'qital' that is, engaging in war at God's behest at the time of aggression on the part of the enemies. This jihad is purely in self-defence in order to counter aggression. The literal meaning of jihad is not war. But to fight in self-defence in accordance with God's commandments also involves a struggle; that is why it is also called jihad.

Jihad, meaning war, is however a temporary and circumstantial matter. If in the real sense any need for defence arises only then will armed jihad be launched. If no such severe urgency arises, no armed jihad will take place.

Just calling an action 'jihad' will not morally validate it. The only true jihad is that which is carried out in accordance with Islam. Islamic jihad is, in actual fact, another name for peaceful struggle. This peaceful struggle is sometimes an inward-looking thing, like waging jihad with the self when it takes place at the level of feeling; sometimes it is desired externally, and manifests itself at the physical level through gestures (like kneeling, prostrating oneself before God).

25

Marriage

The Qur'an states: 'They (women) are your garments. And you (men) are their garments.' (Qur'an, 2:187). These words from the holy scriptures define how men and women relate to each other — like body and its garments. Without garments a body is meaningless, and without a body garments are meaningless. The two must go together, for, apart, they have little reason to exist. This symbolizes the closeness of the two sexes in the material and spiritual senses.

What fundamentally determines the rights and duties of men and women in the roles of husbands and wives is the fact that they are partners for life. This basic principle is derived from the *verse* of the Qur'an which says that men and women are part of one another. (Qur'an, 3:195).

Islam being a religion of nature, its teachings are based on simple principles of nature. When these principles are earnestly adhered to, the family becomes a cradle of peace and amity.

When a man and a woman enter into the marital bond, they bring into existence a social unit called the family. Like any other social unit, this requires an organizer or supervisor. For this special role, Islam has chosen man.

Men are the protectors and maintainers of women, because Allah has given the one more (strength) than the other, and because they support them from their means. (Qur'an, 4:39).

Making man the maintainer in no way indicates that to Allah man is superior to woman. This choice is based on man's capacities for management rather than on his superiority. In a democratic system, everyone has been granted an equal status yet when a government is formed, one particular individual is entrusted with supreme political power. This does not mean that this possesser of power is superior to other citizens. In a democratic system, the president or the prime minister has one vote like all the other citizens. Even then in the interest of good management, authority is entrusted to a single individual.

Except for man's role as managers, man and woman have completely equal status. For instance, if a woman kills a man, and the crime is proved, the woman will be required to pay the penalty (Qur'an, 2:178). There is no legal discrimination in the eyes of the Shari'ah between woman and man. The laws applicable to men are also applicable to women.

The Prophet Muhammad was once asked who of all women was the best. He replied, 'One who makes her husband happy when he sees her, who obeys her husband when he asks her for anything and who does not do anything against his will as regards either herself or his wealth.' (An-Nasa'i, *Sunan*, *Kitab an-Nikah*, 6/68). This *hadith* very aptly points out a woman's duties towards her husband.

On the subject of their wives, the Qur'an enjoins men: 'Treat them with kindness; for even if you do dislike them it may well be that you may dislike a thing which God has meant for your own good.' (Qur'an, 4:19).

This teaching means that even if outwardly unpleasant, a wife should not cause aversion, because God has not made anyone imperfect in all respects. All men and women, if deficient in some respects are gifted in other respects.

What is intended by making women obedient to their husbands is to cultivate in them the kind of fine temperament that will make them true partners to their husbands. This will result in a positive and constructive atmosphere at home rather than one of confrontation and discord. An obedient wife wins the heart of her husband and thus gains the upperhand. Hers is the highest place at home. A disobedient wife on the contrary keeps quarrelling with her husband so that her whole life in consequence is marred with bitterness.

So far as men are concerned, Islam aims at cultivating fair mindedness on all occasion. Being the maintainer of the house, the man should not lose sight of the fact that after death he will be faced with the greatest of the Lords and Masters. There he will not be able to justify himself for being hard to those who were under him in the world. While those who were kind to people under them will be given kind treatment by Allah. Here is a *hadith* to this effect, related by 'Aishah: The Prophet said, 'The best of you is one who is best for his family, and I am best of all of you for my family.'

The rights of men and women, in reality, are not a matter of legal lists, but rather it is a matter of good living.

Islam wants both the man and the woman to acknowledge natural realities. Both should keep their eyes on their responsibilities rather than on their rights. Both should attach real importance to the common goal (the proper maintenance of the family system) rather than on their own selves, and should be ever willing to make any personal sacrifice aimed at this goal.

MARRIAGE SERMON

In the name of Allah, the Compassionate, the Merciful.

O Mankind, have fear of your Lord, who created you from a single soul. From that some He created its mate, and through them He scattered the earth with countless men and women and fear Allah, in whose name you claim (your rights) of one another, and of the ties of kinship. Allah is ever watching you (4:1).

Believers, fear Allah as you rightly should, and when death comes, die true Muslims (3:102).

26

Mercy of God

The Qur'an tells us that the prophets were sent to the world to teach the ways of mercy and compassion.

According to one of the Prophet's sayings, related in the *Sahih* (authentic traditions) of Imam Muslim, "God has a hundred mercies, one of which He has sent down amongst jinn and men and cattle and beasts of prey. With this they are kind and merciful to one another and the wild creature inclines to tenderness to her offspring. The remaining ninety-nine mercies have been reserved by God Himself, so that He may show mercy to His servants on the Day of Resurrection."

This *hadith* is quite specific about the importance of mercy in the eyes of God who is All-Merciful. All of God's creation is, in fact, an expression of divine mercy. And it is this self-same virtue that God desires to see in the hearts of human beings. According to another tradition, the Prophet observed: "Be merciful to people on earth and God on high will be merciful to you." This is the basis of a divine code of ethics in accordance with which man too should have feelings of well-wishing and compassion for others. Everyone should look with sympathy for his fellow men, and remain sensitive to their needs. The relation of one man to another should be that of love—not of hatred, or rivalry, and people should consider it a matter of the greatest good fortune that they are able to serve others.

According to yet another hadith, God said: "My mercy prevails over My anger." Man would do well to adopt this same divine ethics. That is, in social interaction, when one individual has an unpleasant experience with another, he should not permit his feelings of anger and revenge to be aroused. What, ideally, he should do is allow his sense of mercy to prevail over his ire. He would thus refrain from taking any step towards injuring others.

The culture desired by God in human society being that of mercy (*rahmat*), the spirit of tolerance should be predominant in all aspects of human behaviour. People have a feeling of mercy in their hearts for one another which should manifest itself at all times in their conversations and transactions.

An individual—so tradition has it—once came to the Prophet and asked him for some masterly piece of advice which would enable him to tackle the problems of life with greater efficacy. The Prophet replied, 'Don't get angry.' This wise counsel meant that human beings should live together like brothers, friends. Even the most galling of situations should not provoke them. Regardless of the circumstance they should never abandon this culture of *rahmat*.

It is repeatedly stated in the Qur'an that everything in the universe is subservient to the will of God. That being so, the universe, displaying as it does all the various manifestations of His will, His likes and His dislikes, presents the perfect model for human behaviour. It is up to man to adopt this model in his daily living.

What is this example set by the universe? It is one of the perpetual benefit to man, without receiving anything in return. The sun gives light and heat to the whole world without demanding a price for it. At all times and in all places, the atmosphere supplies oxygen free of cost. The trees provide an abundance of fruits and flowers on a strictly unilateral basis. God's provision of rains on such an enormous scale is a vital system on which human life rests. But this natural system of rainfall never sends a bill to man for its services. Even if the universe is abused by man, it does not lose its beneficent character.

This God-given model has to be followed by man

here on earth. The Qur'an puts a question to people: Do they want a religion other than that established by God... although the earth and the heavens have all submitted to Him. It must be conceded that the religion of man and the universe is but one, its greatest features being peace, mercy and magnanimity.

This culture of *rahmat* approved by God is not limited only to human beings, but extends also to the animal world: we must be equally sympathetic to animals. The hadith gives us many guidelines on how to look after animals and treat them with fairness. These are duties laid down by God. One who is cruel to animals risks depriving himself of God's mercy.

On this subject, many traditions have been recorded in the books of *hadith*. Two of these sayings of the Prophet are of particular significance. One concerns a woman who trussed up a cat with rope and deprived it of food and water. Ultimately, the cat died. God so strongly disapproved of this that, in spite of her great devotions (she used to pray a lot), He decreed that she be cast into hell. The other incident concerns a woman who although not religious, took pity on a dog she found lying on the ground, dying of thirst. There was a well nearby, but she had nothing with which to draw water from it. Then she thought of her shawl. She lowered this into the well, then squeezed the water which it soaked up into the mouth of the dog. She continued to do so until its thirst was quenched. The animal's life was thus saved. God was so pleased with this human gesture of mercy that He decreed that she should enter paradise.

Mornings and Evenings

*I*slam is a complete programme for life covering the individual's entire existence. From morning till evening not a single moment of the believer's life excludes the sphere of Islam. It is only after saying his prayers that he goes to bed at night and when he wakes up early in the morning, he first of all purifies his body. After performing his ablutions he says his *fajr* (dawn) prayer. This is the beginning of the God-oriented life which starts with purity and worship. The ensuing hours between morning and noon are meant for economic activities. However, during this period too a believer remembers God constantly. In all matters he adheres strictly to the limits set by God, and in his dealings with people, he is scrupulously honest; in any kind of interaction with others he displays a truly Islamic character.

Then comes the time for the *zuhr* (noon) prayer, which is observed in the afternoon. During the prayer the believer renews his attachment to God as a matter of worship. After purifying his body and his spirit he is again ready to join in life's struggle. And conducting himself throughout as a man of principle, he engages himself in his worldly activities until the time of *asr* (evening) prayer. He again turns to God in prayer to receive his share in God's blessings so that this may afford him assistance in the next stage of life.

In this way a believer passes his time until the sun sets and the moment comes for the fourth prayer, called the *maghrib* prayer at sunset. Once again the believer, abandoning all his activities, turns to God in worship, says the prayer as prescribed, and receives his religious and spiritual sustenance from it. After that, armed with the religious spirit, he again finds himself busy in meeting his worldly requirements. Now the time comes for the fifth prayer called *isha* (night prayer). After saying this prayer, the believer goes to bed and, reckoning up his activities of the day he goes to sleep in order that he may make a better start the next morning when he wakes up.

The Mosque

What is the role of the mosque in Islam? 'Masjid,' or mosque, literally means 'a place for self-prostration,' that is, a place formally designated for the saying of prayers. According to a. *hadith*, the Prophet of Islam observed: "The masjid is a house of God-fearing people." This means, in effect, that it is a centre for the inculcation of reverence, where individuals learn what is meant by piety and are thus prepared for a life of devotion to the Almighty.

The Masjid is built so that people may visit it to read the Book of God, to remember their Creator, silently and in prayer, and to hear His commandments on how they should lead their lives, that is, how to conduct themselves according to His will.

The most important of all these activities is the saying of prayers, a ritual to be carried out five times a day as prescribed by Islam. This act of worship, the greatest means of instilling a sense of awe in the devotee, may be carried out at any place, but ideally, is performed in an organized manner, in congregation, within the mosque. There the worshippers range themselves in orderly rows behind a single prayer leader, the Imam. (The acceptance by the group of just one individual to lead the congregation avoids any dissension which might arise from there being more than one.) The number of the worshippers may be ten or ten thousand: all have to stand in rows behind the Imam. This teaches the lesson of unity. Nevertheless, namaz, in essence, is an individual action. Everyone recites his own prayer and is rewarded on account of its innate rectitude and sincerity.

The prayer begins with ablution, that is, with the washing of the face, hands and feet. This bodily cleansing is a symbolic reminder that the Muslim should lead his life in this world in a state of purification of the feelings and the soul.

What is recited during prayer consists either of verses from the Qur'an or *dhikr*, remembrance of God, and dua, invocation and supplications. All of this is aimed at bringing about a spiritual awakening such as will induce the worshipper to renounce his life of ignorance and heedlessness in favour of a life inspired by Islamic moral values.

Throughout the prayer (*salat*) the phrase, 'Allahu-

Akbar', 'God is great,' is repeated several times. Implicit in these words is the idea that the person uttering them is not great. Their frequent repetition is a lesson in modesty, designed to rid the worshipper of arrogance and egoism, and turn him into a humble servant of God.

The acts of kneeling down and self-prostration are also repeated several times in the course of the prayer, in symbolic submission before God. In this way, the worshipper is conditioned by *salat* to surrender himself to his Maker in all humility.

The various postures in the *salat* climax in the act of self-prostration—the ultimate demonstration of submission. Real proof of this submission to God will only become manifest, however, in subsequent dealings with other human beings, in which it is clear that self-glorification has been replaced by glorification of the Almighty, and that feelings of superiority have given way to profound humility.

The *salat* ends with each worshipper turning his face sideways and uttering these words: "May God's peace and blessings be upon you." Every day, all around the globe, Muslims perform this rite. It is as if they were saying to their fellow men all over the world: "O people, we have no feelings for you but those of peace. Your lives, property and honour—all are safe." It is this spirit with which worshippers are enthused before they return to society.

Besides the five daily obligatory prayers, there is a weekly Friday prayer which is necessarily offered in the mosque. In practice and content it is just like any other prayer, but since a larger number of people gather on this occasion, a sermon (*khutba*), giving religious guidance, is also preached by the Imam before the prayers begin. In this, he reminds worshippers of their accountability to God, of the commandments pertaining to Islamic character and of the proper way to deal with others in society. In this way, the Friday sermon refreshes the memory on religious commitments.

The mosque, initially intended as a place of worship, has come to be built to serve other related purposes, such as housing the madrasa, library, lecture hall, guest house and dispensary etc. According to a hadith the Prophet advised the building of mosques in a simple style, so that there should be no dissipation or dilution of the true religious and spiritual atmosphere.

All mosques (with the exception of three) are of equal religious standing, whether large or small, plainly conceived or architecturally magnificent. The three mosques which have a greater degree of sanctity because of their historical and religious associations are the Masjid-eHaram in Mecca, Prophet's mosque in Medina and the Dome of the Rock in Jerusalem.

Neighbours

Neighbours are our nearest companions. After family members, it is neighbours one comes in contact with. Developing good relations with neighbours is therefore an important aspect of a God-oriented life.

A neighbour, be he a co-religionist or an adherent of another religion, be he of one's own community or of another, must always to be taken good care of. He must be given his dues at all events, according to the demands of the shariah and of humanity.

According to a hadith, the Prophet of Islam observed, "By God, anyone who is a threat to his neighbour is no believer."

According to this hadith, if a Muslim becomes a source of trouble to his neighbours, his faith itself will become suspect.

The humanity of a person and the first criterion of his religiosity and spirituality are tested by the way he behaves towards his neighbours. The relationship with a neighbour serves as a test of whether a person has human feelings or not, and whether he is sensitive to Islamic teachings or not.

If a person's neighbours are happy with him, that is a proof of his being a good man, but if his neighbours are unhappy with him, that is a proof that his behaviour leaves much to be desired.

The commands in the shariah regarding neighbours indicate that a believer must make concessions to his neighbours unilaterally. That is, by doing good to them even if they are ill-behaved towards him.

Being a good neighbour is the first step towards becoming a good human being. It is the good neighbour who will find a share in God's blessings in the Hereafter.

30

Non Violence

Islam is a religion which teaches non-violence. According to the Qur'an, God does not love *fasad*, violence. What is meant here by *fasad* is clearly expressed in verse 205 of the second *surah*. Basically, *fasad* is that action which results in disruption of the social system, causing huge losses in terms of lives and property.

Conversely, we can say with certainty that God loves non-violence. He abhors violent activity being indulged in human society, as a result of which people have to pay the price with their possessions and lives. This is supported by other statements in the Qur'an. For instance, we are told in the Qur'an that peace is one of God's names (59:23). Those who seek to please God are assured by verse 5 of the sixteenth *surah* that they will be guided by Him to "the paths of peace." Paradise, which is the final destination of the society of God's choice, is referred to in the Qur'an as "the home of peace" (89:30), etc.

The entire spirit of the Qur'an is in consonance with this concept. For instance, the Qur'an attaches great importance to patience. In fact, patience is set above all other Islamic virtues with the exceptional promise of reward beyond measure. (39:10)

Patience implies a peaceful response or reaction, whereas impatience implies a violent response. The word *sabr* exactly expresses the notion of non-violence as it is understood in modern times. That patient action is non-violent action has been clearly expressed in the Qur'an. According to one tradition, the Prophet of Islam observed: God grants to *rifq* (gentleness) what he does not grant to *unf* (violence). (*Sunan*, Abu Dawood, 4/255)

The word *rifq* has been used in this *hadith* as an antithesis to *unf*. These terms convey exactly what is meant by violence and non-violence in present times. This *hadith* clearly indicates the superiority of the non-violent method.

God grants on non-violence what He does not grant to violence is no simple matter. It has very wide and deep implications. It embodies an eternal law of nature. By the very law of nature all bad things are associated with violence, while all good things are associated with non-violence.

Violent activities breed hatred in society, while non-violent activities elicit love. Violence is the way of destruction while non-violence is the way of construction. In an atmosphere of violence, it is enmity which flourishes, while in an atmosphere of non-violence, it is friendship which flourishes. The method of violence gives way to negative values while the method of non-violence is marked by positive values. The method of violence embroils people in problems, while the method of non-violence leads people to the exploiting of opportunities. In short, violence is death, non-violence is life.

Both the Qur'an and the hadith have attached great importance to *jihad*. What is *jihad*? *Jihad* means struggle, to struggle one's utmost. It must be appreciated at the outset that this word is used for non-violent struggle as opposed to violent struggle. One clear proof of this is the verse of the Qur'an (25:52) which says: Perform *jihad* with this (i.e. the word of the Qur'an) most strenuously.

The Qur'an is not a sword or a gun. It is a book of ideology. In such a case performing *jihad* with the Qur'an would mean an ideological struggle to conquer peoples' hearts and minds through Islam's superior philosophy.

In the light of this verse of the Qur'an, *jihad* in actual fact is another name for peaceful activism or non-violent activism. Where *qital* is violent activism, *jihad* is non-violent activism.

Non-violence therefore should never be confused with inaction or passivity. Non-violence is action in the full sense of the word. Rather it is more forceful an action than that of violence. It is a fact that non-violent activism is more powerful and effective than violent activism.

Non-violent activism is not limited in its sphere. It is a course of action which may be followed in all matters.

Whenever individuals, groups or communities are faced with a problem, one way to solve it is by resorting to violence. The better way is to attempt to solve the problem by peaceful means, avoiding violence and confrontation. Peaceful means may take various forms. In fact, it is the nature of the problem which will determine which of these peaceful methods is applicable to the given situation.

Peaceful Beginning

When the Qur'an began to be revealed, the first verse of the revelation conveyed the injunction: 'Read!' (*Iqra*) (96:1). By perusing this verse we learn about the initiation of Islamic action. It begins from the point where there is hope of continuing the movement along peaceful lines, and not from that point where there are chances of its being marred by violence.

When the command of *'Iqra'* was revealed, there were many options available in Mecca as starting points for a movement. For instance, one possible starting point was to launch a movement to purify the Kabah of the 360 idols installed in it. But, by pursuing such a course, in such a case the Islamic movement would certainly have had to face a violent reaction from the Quraysh. An alternative starting point could have been an attempt to secure a seat in the Dar-al-Nadwa (Mecca's parliament). At that time almost the whole of Arabia was under the direct or indirect influence of the Roman and Sasanid empires. If the freeing of Arabia from this influence had been made the starting point, this would also have been met with an immediate violent reaction on the part of the Quraysh.

Leaving aside these options, the path followed was that of reading the Qur'an, an activity that could be with certainty continued along peaceful lines: no violent reaction would ensue from engaging in such an activity.

The Prophet of Islam followed this principle throughout his life. His policy was that of adopting non-violent methods in preference to violent methods. It is this policy which was referred to by Aishah, the Prophet's wife, in these words: Whenever the Prophet had to opt for one of two ways, he almost always opted for the easier one. (*Fathul Bari* 6/654)

What are the advantages of non-violent activism over violent activism? They are briefly stated as under:

1. According to the Qur'an there are two faculties in every human being which are mutually antipathetic. One is the ego, and the other is the conscience called respectively *nafs ammara* and *nafs lawwama*. (The Qur'an, 12:53; 75:26) What the violent method invariably does is to awaken the ego which necessarily results in a breakdown of social equilibrium. On the other hand, non-violent activism awakens the conscience. From this results an awakening in people of introspection and self-appraisal. And according to the Qur'an, the miraculous outcome of this is that "he who is your enemy will become your dearest friend." (41:34)

2. A great advantage of the non-violent method is that, by following it, no part of one's time is wasted. The opportunities available in any given situation may then be exploited to the fullest extent—as happened after the no-war pact of Hudaybiya. This peace treaty enabled the energies of the believers to be utilised in peaceful constructive activities instead of being dissipated in a futile armed encounter. One great harm done by violent activism is the breaking of social traditions in the launching of militant movements. Conversely, the great benefit that accrues from non-violent activism is that it can be initiated and prolonged with no damage to tradition.

Generally speaking, attempts to improve or replace

existing systems by violent activism are counter-productive. One coup d'état is often the signal for a series of coups and counter-coups, none of which benefit the common man. The truly desirable revolution is that which permits gradual and beneficial changes. And this can be achieved only on the basis of non-violence.

31

Observing Silence

The Prophet of Islam once observed "One who believes in God and the Last Day should either speak words of goodness or keep quiet."

It is true that failure to speak up and tell the truth when the occasion calls for it can (according to a hadith) earn one the name of 'dumb Satan.' But, there are many occasions when observing silence is more proper and more important.

One example of how essential it is to observe silence is provided by an incident at the battle of Uhud in which the Prophet having been injured in battle, had fallen down in a cave, away from the eyes of the people. His enemies proclaimed that he had been killed, and confusion prevailed among the companions.

In the meantime, a companion of the Prophet caught sight of him and exclaimed, 'Here is the Prophet.' At that moment the Prophet motioned to him to keep quiet (so that the enemy would remain ignorant of his being alive).

Another instance is the hadith which says that asking the assembly to keep quiet while the Imam is giving a sermon is an absurd act. (That would amount to making noise.)

Observing silence at individual meetings too is a good principle to follow, but when the matter pertains to the whole community it assumes an even greater importance. At a delicate moment the observance of silence by a leader can check a riot from taking place. While an ill-timed speech by a leader can lead to a full scale riot, leaving in its wake the loss of hundreds of innocent lives and property worth crores of rupees burnt to ashes. It is in this sense that sister Consolata has observed:

"The greatest number of failings in a community comes from breaking the rule of silence."

On the Occasion of Differences

Differences are a part of life. A divergence of views and behaviour arises between people for a variety of reasons. Just as differences occur among unbelievers and apostates. Similarly differences occur between sincere and pious people. But even if differences cannot be prevented, that is no reason for any individual to indulge in negative behaviour. It should be borne in mind that despite differences, positive behaviour is both a possibility and a necessity.

Regarding a person as being wrong about everything just because he holds different opinions and calling him a hypocrite, bad intentioned and insincere are entirely un-Islamic reactions. The true believer looks at the issue of difference as a matter of intentions, and limits any ensuing dissension to the sphere of its origin. He never allows matters to escalate.

Severing relationships due to differences is not in accordance with the spirit of Islam. Mutual relationships should be maintained while continuing serious discussion of contentious issues. Not greeting the person with whom one has differences or refusing to meet such a person is highly improper.

In this present world everything is designed to put man to the test. Differences also serve this purpose. Man ought to be extremely cautious, particularly at moments of contention. He should continuously strive to be tolerant lest he show some improper reaction, which would be displeasing to God.

Remaining impartial in the face of differences is indeed a difficult task. But its reward too is great. Every right act is treated as an act of worship in Islam; it is therefore an act of superior worship when, in spite of controversies one keeps one's heart free of enmity and vengefulness and adheres strictly to the path of justice.

The emergence of difference is not in itself a bad thing. What is bad is that at the time of differences arising the individuals concerned do not rise to the occasion. They fail miserably in the divine test. Remaining within the confines of taqwa (fear of God) at times of conflict is a great Islamic act, and crossing the boundaries at such moments is an un-Islamic act of the worst degree.

33

Patience
(Sabr)

*P*atience is the exercise of restraint in trying situations. It is a virtue which enables the individual to proceed towards worthy goals, undeflected by adverse circumstances or repeated provocations. If he allows himself to become upset by opposition, taunts or other kinds of unpleasantness, he will never reach his goals. He will simply become enmeshed in irrelevancies.

The only way to deal with the irksome side of daily living is to exercise patience. Patience will ensure that whenever one has some bitter experience, he will opt for the way of tolerance rather than that of reaction to provocation. It will enable one to absorb shocks and to continue, undeterred, on one's onward journey.

Patience, as well as being a practical solution to the problems faced in the outside world, is also a means of positive character building. Failure to exercise patience, gives free rein to negative thoughts and feelings, resulting in the development of a negative personality. While one who remains patient is so morally bolstered by his own positive thoughts and feelings that he develops a positive personality.

Sabr is no retreat. *Sabr* only amounts to taking the initiative along the path of wisdom and reason as opposed to the path of the emotions. Sabr gives one the strength to restrain one's emotions in delicate situations and rather to use one's brains to find a course of action along result-oriented lines.

The present world is fashioned in such a way that everyone is necessarily confronted with unpleasant matters at one time or another. Things which are unbearable have somehow to be borne; harrowing events have to be witnessed and all kinds of pain have to be suffered. In such situations, succumbing to impatience leads to the kind of unnecessary emotional involvement which is counter-productive, while a demonstration of patience has a healing, beneficial effect, allowing one to tread the path of discreet avoidance. Success in the present world is destined only for those who adopt the path of patience in adverse circumstances.

34

Peace

A believer is necessarily a lover of peace. In his mind faith and a desire for peace are so closely interlinked that, regardless of the circumstances, he will strive to the utmost for the maintenance of peace. He will bear the loss of anything else, but the loss of peace he will not endure.

The life that the true believer desires in this world can be lived only in the propitious atmosphere which flowers in conditions of peace. Conditions of unrest breed a negative atmosphere which to him is abhorrent.

But if peace is to be maintained, it calls for a certain kind of sacrifice. That is, when conditions become disturbed, the believer must overlook both the misdeeds leading up to this situation and the identity of the wrongdoers. He must suffer all the harm and injustice done to him without making any attempt either to retaliate, or to bring the miscreants to book, so that a state of peace should continue to prevail. The believer has to be willing to pay this price, so that his pursuance of constructive ends should proceed unhampered.

The believer is like a flower in the garden of nature. Just as a hot wind will shrivel up a bloom and cause it to die, so will constant friction distract the believer from achieving positive goals. And just as a cool breeze will enable the flower to retain its beauty for its natural life-span, so will a peaceful atmosphere enable the believer to fulfil the obligations of divine worship in a spirit of great serenity. Peace is thus central to the life of the believer.

Islam is a religion of peace. And peace is a universal law of nature. That is because God loves the condition of peace, and disapproves of any state of unrest. God's predilection for peace is quite enough reason for the believer also to love peace. In no circumstances will the true believer ever tolerate the disruption of peace.

Piety

Taqwa means piety, that is, leading a life of caution and restraint in this world.

Umar Farooq, the second Caliph once asked a companion of the Prophet what *taqwa* was. He replied, "O leader of the believers, have you ever crossed a path which has thorny shrubs on both sides?" But the companion instead of replying asked another question, "What did you do on such an occasion?" Umar Farooq replied, "I gathered my clothes close to me and moved ahead cautiously." The companion said, "Now I know what is meant by *taqwa*."

The present world is a testing ground. Here, various kinds of thorns have been scattered for the purpose of testing man, such as negativity, false issues raised by non-serious people, the lure of worldly things. Besides these, there are many unpleasant occurrences which disturb people's minds and lead them away from the path of virtue.

All these things are like thorny shrubs lining both sides of the path of life. At any moment it is feared that man may embroil himself in these thorns and then instead of going forward, remain entrapped in these snares of life.

In such a state of affairs the wise man is one who travels the paths of life by gathering up his clothes to avoid becoming entangled in these unpleasant snares. In this way, he is able to continue his journey unhampered. Yet at all times he must remain conscious of the fact that he must protect himself. He has to adopt the path of avoidance, not of entanglement.

Man has been created with an upright nature. If no hindrance comes in the way, then every man will, on his own, take the right course. That is why, the utmost precaution must be taken against allowing unnatural obstacles to come in the way.

Then, guided by this upright nature, man will continue to walk along the right path until he meets his Lord.

36

Plants

Vegetation and plants has been described in the Qur'an as a special blessing of God. According to the Qur'an Paradise is a world of highest quality, where the believers, God's favoured servants, will be inhabited. This abode has been called Paradise, meaning a garden, which is a special feature of paradise, referred to in the Qur'an as 'beautiful mansions in Gardens of eternity." (61:12)

A believer is God's desired person. What this desired person is like. In the Qur'an he has been likened to a tree (14:24). This is a very meaningful simile. As we all know man receives shade, fruits and flowers from the tree. The sight of a green tree cools the eyes of the people. All such qualities should be found in God worshippers. Human beings should live in society in a manner that they may give comfort to everyone, they may benefit everyone, they may become a source of coolness to all.

There is a hadith to this effect. The Prophet of Islam said: The believer is like a gentle plant. When the winds blow it does not show haughtiness, instead it swerves to and fro with the wind, and when the winds are not blowing it stands in position once again. Exactly the same is the case with the God worshipper. A true believer lives among the people with gentleness. He does not display arrogance. His way is that of adjustment and not of clash and confrontation. He follows the principle of persuasion and avoids the way of violence.

At one point in the Qur'an honey has been mentioned in particular. Honey a valuable drink is produced from the plants. The Qur'an tells us about honey that 'therein is healing for men' (16:69. This indicates symbolically that besides food and drink plants have another special quality that of having the healing effect. It is a fact that most of the medicine are produced from plants. This healing attributes of the plants is so great that even when a tiger, a carnivorous animal, takes ill, he eats grass to cure himself. So God has granted us double blessings in the form of plants. They serve both as food and as medicine.

The Qur'an repeatedly mentions plants as a special blessings of God. Here are some verses in this regard:

Mentioning the initial stage of creation the Qur'an states that "after creating the earth God drew out therefrom its water and its pasture" (79:31). Water and vegetation are closely related to one another without water vegetation cannot come into existence. This precious vegetation is available nowhere in the vast expanses of the universe but on earth. That is why the existence of the living things too exist only on earth, because the existence of life is not possible without vegetation. A verse in the Qur'an is as follows:

"Then let man look at his food (and how we provide it) for that we pour forth water in abundance. And we split the earth in fragments. And produce therein grain, and grapes and the fresh vegetation, and olives and dats, and enclosed gardens, dense with lofty trees, and fruits and fodder, a provision for you and your cattle" (80:23-24).

This shows that God has made the vegetation as special food for both men and animals. Through vegetation human body receives all its necessary requirements which are essential for biological existence. Alongwith it such elements too are placed in vegetation as produce resistance to various ailments. Furthermore God has also added varied tastes to these vegetation so that these serve not only as simple food but also as tasty food. Here is a verse in the Qur'an:

"It is He who produced gardens with creepers and without, and dates, and seed produce of all kinds, and olives and pomegranates, similar (in kind) and different (in variety). Eat of their fruit in their season, but render the dues that are proper on the day that the harvest is gathered. But waste not by excess. For God loves not the wasters" (6:142)

This verse mentions vegetables, fruits and dry-fruits. We are told that God has made all these things to serve as food for man. God desires that man should receive these food products by farming and gardening. Then alongwith eating them himself he should also feed others and thank God for His blessings.

According to the Qur'an, from various aspects, farming and gardening are means of human existence, these provide both spiritual as well as physical food for man.

The Prophet of Islam observed: when a person plants a tree and the tree grows and yields fruit, then human beings and birds eat its fruit, this will be an act of charity on the part of the planter of the tree.

In a similar vein there is another hadith. The Prophet once observed: "If you have a plant in your hand and you can see the Doomsday approaching, even then, without any further delay, you should put the plant in the earth.

Such traditions show how great importance is attached to vegetation in Islam. In this way Islam produces the spirit in man that he should make earth a green, verdant to the extent that even if there is fear that after his plantation an earthquake was to come and the earth was going to be destroyed in its wake. This is the education of plantation for the sake of plantation.

37

Prayer

*P*rayer is worship of God. It is obligatory for the believer to pray five times a day. These prayers are performed in mosques in congregation.

But prior to the performance of prayer comes *wudu*, ablution. In ablution the hands, face, and feet are washed with water. This washing in order to cleanse awakens the feeling in man that he should always lead a life of purity. Then by uttering the words 'God is Great' he enters into the act of *salat*. This is to acknowledge that all greatness belongs to God. Thus the proper attitude for man is to lead a life of modesty and humility.

By reciting some parts from the Qur'an in prayer, the devotee refreshes his memory about God's commandments regarding himself. Then he kneels and prostrates himself before God, in physical expression of the idea that the only course that befits him is to lead his life as a submissive servant of God.

The prayer is concluded by turning the face first to the right side, then to the left, and uttering the words 'Assalamu-alaykum' (Peace and blessings of God be upon you). This is a demonstration of the fact that, spiritually conditioned by prayer, the devotees are now entering into the world with no other thoughts and feelings in their minds but those of mercy towards others, and peace for all mankind. Prayer turns their resolve to remain peaceful members of society, and to harbour no ill feelings towards anyone.

Prayer in one respect is the worship of God, and in another it is an acknowledgement of the divinity of God. It is to surrender before God, attributing all kinds of greatness to Him alone.

In yet another respect, prayer prepares the individual to lead a worthy life among people, adopting an attitude of modesty, sympathy and good-will in all his dealings. In short, prayer perfects man's relation with God as well as with other human beings.

Promise

In mutual dealings in social life, it often happens that a person gives his word to another. There is apparently no third person or group between the two, yet there is always a third present and that is God who is the supreme witness. That is why every promise becomes a divine promise.

A believer therefore is extremely sensitive about giving his word. His conviction is that every commitment made between two persons is under the watchful eyes of God, and that he will be accountable for its fulfilment in the court of God. This compels him to be highly responsible as regards his promises. Whenever he gives his word to anyone he makes a point of keeping it.

People who invariably fulfil their promises are predictable characters in a society, and give their society that particular quality which exists on a vast scale throughout the universe. Every part of this universe is functioning with the most exact precision. For instance, we can learn in advance about any star's or planet's rotation and where it will be moving after a hundred or even a thousand years. Similarly, we know in advance what the boiling point of water will be. In this way the entire universe evinces a predictable character.

Many other virtues come in the wake of the regular fulfilment of promises. One of these is mutual trust. In a society where mutual trust exists, there is no discord and dissension between the people; there is an atmosphere of confidence and peaceability as there is no fear of promises being broken.

Readiness to fulfil promises is a commendable trait; it is *iman* (faith) that makes man the possessor of this highest of human virtues.

Prophet

A prophet is a person chosen by God as His representative. When God appoints someone as His Messenger, He sends His angel to him to inform him of his new status. In that way, the individual can have no doubts about his appointment as God's apostle. Later, God reveals His message to him through His angels, so that he may communicate the divine teachings to all his fellow men.

God has given man a mind so that he may be endowed with understanding. But this mind can only grasp things that are apparent. It cannot go below the surface, and there are many things to be apprehended, for which a superficial knowledge is insufficient. The deeper realities of this world are beyond the scope of the human mind, and so far as God and the next world are concerned, they must remain forever invisible—beyond the reach of human perception.

What the Prophet does is to enlighten people so that

they may overcome this human inadequacy. He tells of the reality of things here and now, and also gives tidings of the next world. He thereby enables the individual to formulate a plan for his entire existence in the full light of knowledge and awareness so that he may carve out a successful life for himself.

Since the settlement of human beings on earth, the prophets have been coming one after another. In every age they have been the conveyors of God's messages to human beings. However, whatever records of these ancient prophets have survived have been rendered historically unreliable by interpolations. The same is true of the books they brought to mankind. The sole exception was the case of the Prophet Muhammad, who had been chosen by God as His Final Messenger. The Prophet was born in an age when the history of the world was already being extensively chronicled. This in itself made circumstances conducive to authentic records being kept of God's messages and the Prophet's exemplary life. The relevant facts were passed on from one generation to the next by both oral and written tradition, and with the advent of the printing press came the modern guarantee that no changes would ever be made in the divine scriptures. This renders unassailable the position of the Prophet Muhammad (upon whom be peace) as God's Final Messenger and His sole representative on earth till Doomsday.

Prophethood

Human destiny, by Islamic lights, is a matter of man having been placed on this earth by God, so that he may be put to the test—the test being of his capacity to make correct moral choices. It is for this purpose that man has been given complete freedom, for without such freedom, the divine test would have no meaning, no validity.

It is required of man that he should lead his life on earth following a regimen of strict self-discipline. Wherein should he find the guiding principles for such a course? The answer, according to Islam, is in prophethood. Throughout the history of mankind, God appointed certain human beings—prophets—who would be the recipients and conveyors of His guidance as sent through His angels. The last in the series was the Prophet Muhammad.

The concept of prophethood is totally different from that of incarnation. According to the latter concept, God

Himself is re-born in human shape on earth in order to give succour to humanity. Propehthood, according to Islam, is of quite another order of being. A prophet in the Islamic sense is a man, just like any other human being: his uniqueness resides solely in his also being a messenger of God.

A messenger is not an 'inspired' person in the simple sense of the word. By Islamic tenets, prophethood is dependent not on inspiration, but on divine revelation. Inspiration is a common psychological phenomenon, of the kind experienced by a poet, whereas revelation is a true and direct divine communication. It was consciously sent and also consciously received by the Prophet. The Qur'an is a collection of these divine revelations, which the Prophet received over a period of 23 years.

According to Islam, prophethood is not acquired but God-given. That is, it is not possible to engage in spiritual exercises and then, as a result, be elevated to prophethood. Not even the Prophet had any say in this matter of selection. The choice depends upon God alone.

The Prophet's responsibility was to communicate the divine message to humanity. In doing so, if he received a negative response from the people, or even in extreme cases was presecuted, he had nevertheless to follow a strict policy of avoidance of confrontation, and had unilaterally to adopt the path of patience and forbearance. He was responsible only in so far as the conveying of the message was concerned. As for the response to, or acceptance of the message, that entirely depended on the addressees. But clearly, the greater the number who accepted the message, the greater the sphere in which a practical system of guidance sent by God became established.

The Qur'an testifies to the fact that God's messengers came in every age and in every region. According to a hadith, more than one lakh messengers were sent to guide the people. However, the prophets mentioned by name in the Qur'an are two dozen in number, the Prophet Muhammad being the last of them. In the past, the need for new prophets had always arisen because God's religion, suffering from the vagaries of time, had frequently been distorted from its original form. New prophets had to come to the world time and time again in order to revivify the true spirit of religion, which had been lost when nations in ancient times, entrusted with the guardianship of the divine scriptures, had repeatedly betrayed their trust, allowing the book of God to be laid waste. They had to right the wrongs done by human interpolations in the books they brought with them. But after the Prophet Muhammad, the world will see no further prophets, for the Book which the Prophet gave to the world—the Qur'an—is still perfectly preserved in its original state. In the divine scheme of things, no further prophets are then required.

It is not only the Prophet Muhammad's (upon whom be peace) Scripture which is preserved in its pristine state, but his very spirit, for his utterances, the events of his life, the struggle of his prophetic mission, have all been fully recorded and have remained intact.

The Qur'an tells us that when the Prophet Muhammad proclaimed his prophethood, people found it difficult to believe in him. They asked, "What kind of messenger is this? He eats and drinks and moves about in the markets. If God had to send a prophet, why didn't He send an angel?"

In reply the Qur'an had this to say: 'If the earth had been inhabited by angels, We would have sent an angel as a prophet, but since it is human beings who live on earth, a man has been selected as God's Messenger.'

The Prophet then, as the bearer of God's message, had to project himself as a model for other human beings. The Qur'an, indeed, describes the Prophet as a model character. It was on this consideration that a messenger was selected from amongst human beings. He experienced all that was experienced by others: grief and solace, advantages and disadvantages, pain and pleasure, etc. Yet he never wavered from the truth, thus setting an example of how others must abide by the truth on all occasions. This deprived wrongdoers of the excuse that they had no role model to show them the path which God desired them to follow.

The messenger of God was born just like any other human being. He led his life just as others did. In this way, he clearly demonstrated that the way of life which he exhorted others to lead was entirely practicable. His words and deeds thus became a realistic example of how God's servants should conduct themselves on earth and what path they must opt for to avert God's displeasure and earn God's blessings.

41

Purity of Body and Soul

A believer is a clean person. First of all faith cleanses his soul. Consequently his appearance becomes pure as well. His religious thinking makes him a person who loves cleanliness.

A believer performs his ablutions before praying five times a day by washing his face, hands and feet. He takes a bath daily to purify his body. His clothes may be simple, but he always likes to wear well laundered clothes.

Along with this he likes to keep his home clean. Therefore, he cleans his home daily and keeps all his things in their proper places. All these duties become part of his daily life.

A believer does not rest content until he has set all things right, from his body to his home.

This taste for cleanliness is not limited only to his

home and body. It also extends outside his home to his neighbours. He begins to want his whole environment to be clean, wherever he stays. So he takes special care to see that he and his family members do not defile their surroundings. This training he gives to others as well. Thus he is not satisfied until and unless he has succeeded in bringing into existence a clean atmosphere all around.

For a common person cleanliness is only cleanliness. But for a believer, cleanliness, besides being simply cleanliness is also an act of worship, for he knows that God likes clean and pure persons.

Furthermore, the faith of the believer is a guarantee that when he has cleaned his body his soul is likewise cleaned. That is why at the moment of washing himself clean, he utters these words in prayer: Oh God, purify my inner self along with my outer body. In this way, the earnest prayer makes his soul clean too, like his body.

42

The Qur'an

The Qur'an, the Book of God, enshrines the teachings which were basically the same as were to be found in previous revealed scriptures. But these ancient scriptures are no longer preserved in their original state. Later additions and deletions have rendered them unreliable, whereas the Qur'an, preserved in its original state, is totally reliable.

The Qur'an has 114 chapters. Its contents in a nutshell are: belief in one God, and considering oneself answerable to Him; firm belief that the guidance sent by God through the Prophet Muhammad is the truth and that man's eternal salvation rests thereon.

The position of the Qur'an is not just that it is one of the many revealed scriptures but that it is the only authentic heavenly book, as all other books, due to human additions and deletions, have been rendered historically unreliable. When a believer in the previous revealed scripture turns to the Qur'an, it does not mean that he is rejecting his own belief, but rather amounts to his having re-discovered his own faith in an authentic form.

The Qur'an is a sacred book sent by the Lord of all creation. It is a book for all human beings, because it has been sent by that Divine Being who is the God of all of us.

The Qur'an is no new heavenly scripture. It is only an authentic edition of the previous heavenly scriptures. In this respect, the Qur'an is a book for all human beings, of all nations. It is the expression of God's mercy for one and for all. It is a complete message sent by God for every one of us. The Qur'an is a light of guidance for all the world just as the sun is the source of light and heat for all the world.

Islam means submission. The religion of Islam is so named because it is based on obedience to God. A true believer in Islam is one who subordinates his thinking to God, who follows God's dictates in all aspects of his life.

Islam is the religion of the entire universe. For the entire universe and all its parts are functioning in accordance with the law laid down by God.

Such behaviour is also desired of man. Man should also lead his life as God's obedient servant just as the rest of the universe is fully subservient to God. The only difference is that the universe has submitted to God compulsorily, while man is required to submit to the will of God by his own choice.

When man adopts Islam, first of all it is his thinking which comes under Islam, then his desires, his feelings, his interests, his relations, his loves and his hatred. All are coloured by his obedience to God's will.

When man, in his daily life comes under God's command, his behaviour with people, his dealings, all are molded by the demands of Islam. From inside to outside he becomes a person devoted to God.

Man is God's servant, and indeed, the only proper way for man in this world is to live as the servant of God. Islam, in fact, is another name for this life of servitude to God. Where the Islamic life is devoted to the service of God, the un-Islamic life unashamedly flouts the will of God. Islam teaches man to lead an obedient life and surrender himself completely to the will of God. It is people who do so who will share God's blessings in the next world.

Religion of Peace

The Model World according to Islam, is a world of peace. Islam in itself means a religion of peace. The Qur'an says: And God calls to the home of peace. This is the message of Islam to mankind. It means that 'Build a world of peace on earth so that you may be granted a world of peace in your eternal life in the Hereafter'.

Now what are the basic elements of building of a culture of peace, according to Islam to be brief, these are three—compassion, forgiveness and respect for all.

Let's take compassion first. If you go through the Qur'an and Hadith, you will find many verses in the Qur'an and Hadith which lay great stress on compassion. For instance, the Prophet of Islam said: O people, be compassionate to others so that you may be granted compassion by God.

Thus Islam makes compassion a matter of self-interest for every man. As one's own future depends on one's compassionate behaviour to other fellowmen. In this way Islam motivates us to be compassionate in our dealing with each other. One who wants to receive God's grace will have to show compassion to others.

Let's take forgiveness. The Qur'an has to say this in this regard "when they are angered, they forgive." There are a number of verses in the Qur'an which promote forgiveness.

Then there is a *hadith*. Once a person came to the Prophet and asked him, "O Prophet, give me a master advice by which I may be able to manage all the affairs of my life." The Prophet replied: "Don't be angry." It means that 'forgive people even at provocation.' That is, adopt forgiveness as your behaviour at all times.

Now let's take the third principle—Respect for all. There is a very interesting story, recorded by al-Bukhari in this regard.

The Prophet of Islam once saw a funeral procession passing by a street in Madina. The Prophet was seated at that time. On seeing the funeral the Prophet stood up in respect. At this one of his companions said: 'O Prophet, it was the funeral of a Jew (not a Muslim). The Prophet replied: 'Was he not a human being?' What it meant was that every human being is worthy of respect. There may be differences among people regarding religion and culture, but everyone has to respect the other. For, according to Islam, all men and women are blood brothers and blood sisters. And all are creatures of one and the same God.

These three principles are the basic pillars to form a peaceful society. Wherever these three values are to be found the result no doubt will be a society of peace and harmony.

The above references are enough to show that Islam is a culture of peace. It is true that some Muslims are engaged in violence in the name of Islam. But you will have to differentiate between Islam and Muslims. You have to see Muslims in the light of Islam and not vice versa.

44

The Rights of Human Beings

A believer has important responsibilities towards both God and man. His duty towards God means believing in Him with all His attributes, worshipping Him, regarding himself accountable to Him; and making himself ready to carry out wholeheartedly any such demands that God may make upon him.

Another responsibility of the believer is one which concerns the rights of human beings. This responsibility devolves upon him in his relations with others. Every man or woman, a relative or neighbour, a fellow townsman or compatriot or one with whom he has dealings in business — everyone has some rights over him. It is incumbent upon a believer to fulfil those rights, failing which he will not be deserving of God's succour.

What is meant by recognising the rights of human beings (*Huquq al-Ihad*)? This means that whenever and wherever a believer meets another person, he should give him such treatment as is in accordance with Islamic teachings. He should refrain from such behaviour as does not come up to the standard of Islam.

Examples of proper Islamic behaviour are giving respect to others, never humiliating others while giving them help, acting for the good of others, and if unable to benefit them in any way, at least doing no one any harm, fulfilling trusts, never breaking them; never usurping the wealth and property of others; dealing justly with others regardless of the circumstances; giving the benefit of the doubt to others, not believing in allegations made against others without proper proofs; advising others in earnest.

Everyone has a duty to fulfil these responsibilities towards other human beings according to the Islamic shariah. This is called *Huququl Ibad*, or human rights.

45

Salvation

What is the greatest issue facing man in this world? It is how to secure salvation in the life after death so that he may find his true abode and have a share in God's eternal blessings.

Every man who is born in this present world has to enter another world after death. In this world man was granted life's opportunities as a matter of being tested by them. Whatever man receives in the next world will be purely on the basis of his deeds in this world. This means that in the world before death, man has been given a great number of things and opportunities, whether or not he deserved them. But after death, the criterion of receiving will only be a matter of his just deserts; nothing will be given to him to try him.

This means that those who are held to be deserving will be granted not out of God's blessings but more that they actually merited. But those who have done nothing to deserve God's blessings will have nothing whatsoever in store for them. They will be compelled to live in a state of utter deprivation.

This is man's greatest problem. To what should he give the greatest attention so that he may not be held undeserving in the life to come? Everyone has to himself exert to the utmost in the consciousness that in the next stage of his life he may by default be considered without merit. Then there would be no further scope for him to earn God's blessings, salvation would elude him completely.

The next world is the most perfect and eternal world. There, all kinds of pleasures and happiness have been stored up for mankind. It is that world which man should cherish most, and it should be the place to which he most earnestly aspires. But the time for action to secure a place in that blessing-filled world is not the world after death, but the world before death. The present world is the place for action, while the next world is the place for reaping the reward for one's deeds.

Salvation in the life Hereafter is only for those who prove themselves deserving of it.

46

Signs of God

The Indian writer Khwajah Hasan Nizami (1878-1955) once wrote an article in Urdu entitled "Story of a Fly." In it he complained to a fly about the bother it caused people. "Why don't you let us sleep in peace?" he remonstrated. "The time for sleep and eternal repose has not yet come." the fly replied. "When it does, then you can sleep in peace. Now it is better for you to remain alert and active." This little exchange shows that if one remains open to admonition, one will find a lesson for one's life even in such mundane events as the buzz of a fly. If one's mind is closed, on the other hand, then not even the roar of bombshells and artillery fire will be able to break through its barriers. Only the tempest of the Last Day will bring such people to their senses, but that will not be the time to take heed: that will be a time for retribution, not constructive action.

The Qur'an tells us of one who is admitted to

paradise bringing before God "a sound heart" (26:89). There is a saying of the Prophet to much the same effect. "Whomsoever God wishes good for," he said, "He instructs in religion." Looked at together, these statements show that God's greatest blessing to a person is an open mind and a sound, receptive intellect that sees truth for what it is. Such a mind is free of complexes: it is able to form opinions in a free and unprejudiced spirit. A sound mind does not take long to absorb any truth, or take in any lesson contained in the world at large. The universe is like spiritual sustenance for such a mind, which develops and thrives by deriving nourishment from what it sees, feels and hears in the world around it.

Signs of God are spread all over the universe. In some places it is rocks and inanimate matter that provide a pointer to some profound reality, in others it is "flies"— menial objects—that sound out a message for man. Sometimes God enables one of His servants to call his fellow men to truth in plain, spoken language. In all such instances it is one who has opened his mind to truth who will find it. If one is not receptive to instruction one will gain nothing from all the signs that are scattered throughout the world. An open mind derives instruction even from a "fly", while not even divine revelation and prophetic teachings can break down the barriers of a closed mind.

There is nothing that can take the place of a receptive intellect. One who remains open to instruction will look on the whole world as living proof of divine realities. One who goes through life with a closed mind, however, is like a beast who hears and sees all, but understands nothing.

Simplicity

A believer is one who finds God. God's discoverer starts living by nature on the plane of higher realities. He rises above outward, superficial things and finds sources of interest in the world of piety.

Such a person by his very nature becomes a simplicity loving person. His motto is: Simple living and high thinking.

One who has acquired the taste for the meaning of the divine reality can have no taste for outward and material things. Such a person relishes simplicity. In his eyes pretensions lose their attraction. His soul finds peace in natural things. Unnatural and artificial things appear to him as if they are causing his inner world disintegrate and creating obstacles to the progress of his spiritual journey.

Simplicity is a support to the believer. It contributes to his strength. By opting for simplicity he is able to put his time to the best use by not wasting it on irrelevant matters. He does not let his attention be diverted to things which are inessential so far as his goal is concerned. And in this way he is able to devote himself whole-heartedly to the achievement of higher goals.

Simplicity is the food of the believer, and, having its own internal beauty, it serves as an apparel for his modesty. It is in an atmosphere of simplicity that his personality finds the scope for its growth. On the contrary, if the believer builds up an artificial glamour around himself, he will eventually feel as if he is imprisoned in a cell.

A believer considers himself God's servant in the ultimate sense of the word. His thoughts and feelings are all perfectly attuned to this servitude, to this condition of being God's servant. One who consistently thinks in this way inevitably finds his whole disposition veering towards simplicity. Since ostentation, artificiality and social pretensions are at variance with his disposition, he resolutely avoids them throughout his life, in his manner of living and in his daily dealings.

Social Service

All the teachings of Islam are based on two basic principles -- worship of God and service of men. Without putting both of these principles into practice, there can be no true fulfillment of one's religious duties.

In its followers, Islam inculcates the spirit of love and respect for all human beings. By serving human beings on the one hand they please their God, and on the other they achieve spiritual progress for themselves.

According to a *hadith*, you should be merciful to people on earth and God on high will be merciful to you. In this way Islam links personal salvation to serving others. One can receive God's reward in the Hereafter only if one has done something to alleviate the sufferings of mankind.

According to a *hadith* on Doomsday, God will say to a person, "I was ill, but you did not come to nurse Me." The man will reply, "God, You being the Lord of the universe how can You be ill?" God will answer, "Such and such servant of Mine was ill. Had you gone there, you would have found Me there with him." Then God will say to another person, "I was hungry, but you did not feed Me." The person will reply, "God, You are the Lord of the worlds, how could You go hungry?" God will say, "Such and such of my servant came to you, but you did not feed him. Had you done so, you would have found Me with him." Then God will say to yet another man, "I was thirsty, and you did not give Me water to drink." That person will also say, "God, You are the Lord of the worlds, how could You be thirsty?" God will say, "Such and such servant of Mine came to you, but you did not give him water to drink. Had you offered him water, you would have found Me there with him."

From this, we learn the Islamic principle that if someone wants to find God, he shall first have to make himself deserving of this by helping the poor and the needy. This act becomes a means of spiritual progress for him. And there is no doubt about it that it is only those people who have elevated themselves spiritually, who will find God.

This culture of mercy and compassion approved of by God is not limited to human beings, but extends also to the animal world. We must be equally sympathetic to animals. The Hadith gives us many guidelines on how to look after animals and treat them with fairness. There are duties laid down by God. One who is cruel to animals risks depriving himself of God's mercy.

Social Work

One of the noble feelings that a believer should possess is the urge or desire to come to the assistance of others. He should fulfil their needs without expecting any return.

Coming to the assistance of others is, in essence, an acknowledgement of the blessings which God has showered upon him. It is that person, who helps others who has something more than others. For example, one who has eyes comes to the assistance of one who has not been blessed with the precious gift of sight; an able-bodied person will give physical help to the disabled; a wealthy person will give donations to the poor; the man with resources will come to the aid of one who lacks them, and so on.

On all such occasions when one man helps out another by virtue of those blessings which God has given him, he is in fact showing his gratitude to God for these favours. He is saying within himself, O God, whatever I have is all given by You. Now I am spending it in Your path, I pray You for more blessings and mercy for both of us (the helper and the receiver).

By engaging oneself in social work, one is not only helping another but is actually raising his own moral status. Making use of one's possessions only for oneself is to live on the plane of animals, for the beasts share nothing with others.

Man, superior to all other creatures, lives on a far higher plane. The proper attitude in accordance with his status is not to keep himself to himself but to embrace the whole of humanity. He should lead his life as a well-wisher to all, ready to help everyone, accepting others' rights over his own possessions.

Social work is in other words, service to humanity. And after the worship of God, no task is nobler.

Society

What are the teachings of Islam on the subject of the multi-religious society? When Islam is studied with this question in mind, we find clear commandments in this regard. In chapter 109 of the Qur'an, the Prophet is enjoined to address non-Muslims thus: "I do not worship what you worship, nor do you worship what I worship. I shall never worship what you worship, nor will you ever worship what I worship. You have your own religion and I have mine." This verse of the Qur'an coupled with other of its teachings amounts to an easily applicable formula for mutual respect. It means simply that all believers, whatever their elected religion, must have due reverence for the religions adhered to by others.

What establishes the need for such a formula is the edifice of religion being founded on the total conviction that it is the whole truth. To have any followers at all, a religion must carry that conviction. It is in the nature of things. But religious conviction alone is not a broad enough base on which to form a just society, particularly if that conviction is publicly expressed by different groups through the widely differing practices of different faiths. In the multi-religious context, it also takes broad-mindedness, compassion and fellow feeling. Only when in possession of these virtues can members of society display that tolerance in their dealings with others which will ensure a lasting peace.

The principle of mutual respect is a natural one and is to be found in all areas of civilized living. One of the major demands made by Islam is that this natural principle be upheld and acted upon by the adherents of different religions, so that societal structures may be strengthened by stable and enduring human relationships.

For the greater part of his life, the Prophet of Islam lived in a society where adherents of other religions existed side by side with believers in Islam. The Prophet's behaviour towards the former was invariably that of respect and tolerance.

At a time when the majority of the denizens of Mecca were still idolaters, his conduct consistently conveyed his high moral character. On the one hand, he communicated to them the message of *tawheed* with love and kindness and, on the other, fulfilled all of their human rights. That is why the non-Muslims of Mecca had such great confidence in him—to the point of entrusting their belongings to his care. This they continued to do right up to the last days of his stay in Mecca.

After the attainment of his prophethood, he lived in Mecca for a period of thirteen years, later migrating to Madina, where he lived for ten years until his death. For about half of this period in Madina, he was living among people belonging to three religions — Muslims, Jews and idolators. The Prophet devised a constitution for these people, known in history as *Sahifa-e-Madina* (Madina Charter).

This charter expressly mentioned that issues concerning these three groups domiciled in Madina would be decided on the basis of their own religious traditions — those of Muslims according to their Islamic traditions, and those of idolators and Jews according to their respective traditions. This principle of Islam was intended to apply at all places where Muslims lived along with adherents of other religions. This *sunnat*, or practice of the Prophet, for a plural society carries the same moral authority as other of his practices.

Islam recognises no difference between Muslims and non-Muslims from the ethical standpoint. The rights granted to a Muslim are exactly the same as those granted to a non-Muslim.

A tradition in *Sahih al-Bukhari* gives us a telling example of how this principle should in practice be followed. According to this tradition, when the Prophet was in Madina, he saw a funeral procession passing along a street. The Prophet was seated at that time. On seeing it, the Prophet stood up in deference to the deceased person. One of his companions said: "O God's messenger, it was the funeral of a Jew (not a Muslim)." The Prophet replied: "Was he not a human being?"

This tradition of the Prophet of Islam tells us that every human being is worthy of respect. There might be differences between people in religion, culture and traditions but it is incumbent upon everyone to accord equal respect to other, as all men and women are creatures of one and the same God. All are descendants of Adam and Eve.

Everyone has certainly the right to adopt one religion according to his beliefs. But with that choice comes the ineluctable responsibility of giving respect in full measure to adherents of other faiths and, in the light of those faiths, giving them what is ethically their due.

Speaking the Truth

A believer in God is also necessarily a truth-loving person. He always speaks the truth. In all matters he says just what is in accordance with reality. A true believer cannot afford to tell lies, or hide facts. What does it mean to speak the truth? It is to have no contradiction between man's knowledge and the words that he utters and for that matter, whatever he says should be what has come to his knowledge. Falsehood, by contrast, is the utterance of statements which do not tally with knowledge.

Truth is the highest virtue of a believer's character. A believer is a man of principle. And for such a person telling the truth is paramount. For him no other behaviour is possible, for he finds it impossible to deny the truth.

The world of God is based wholly on truth. Here everything expresses itself in its real form. The sun, the moon, rivers, mountains, stars and planets are all based on truth. They appear just as they really are. In this unfathomably vast universe of God nothing is based on untruth. There is nothing which shows itself in any form other than its real form.

This is the character of nature, which is spread out on a universal scale. A believer too has exactly the same character. He is totally free from falsehood or double-standards. A believer is all truth. His whole existence is moulded to truth. From the very first he appears to be a true person both inside and out.

Speaking the truth is not only a matter of policy for the believer: it is his very religion. Compromising in the matter of truth is not possible for him. He speaks the truth as he cannot live without doing so. He speaks the truth because he knows that not speaking the truth is the negation of his own personality and commitment to something which is the negation of the self is not possible for any worthy person.

Spiritual Uplift

Islam is the answer to the demands of nature. It is in fact a counterpart of human nature. This is why Islam has been called a religion of nature in the Qur'an and Hadith.

A man once came to the Prophet Muhammad and asked him what he should do in a certain matter. The Prophet replied, 'Consult your heart about it.' By the heart the Prophet meant common sense. That is, what one's common sense tells one would likewise be the demand of Islam.

What does human nature desire more than anything? It desires, above all, peace and love. Every human being wants to live in peace and to receive love from the people around him. Peace and love are the religion of human nature as well as the demand of Islam. The Qur'an tells us, "..and God calls to the home of peace." (10:25)

One of the teachings of Islam is that when two or more people meet, they must greet one another with the words, *Assalamu-'Alaikum* (Peace be upon you). Similarly, *Salat* or five times daily prayer is the highest form of worship in Islam. At the close of each prayer all worshippers have to turn their faces to either side and utter the words *Assalamu-'Alaikum wa rahmatullah* (May peace and God's blessings be upon you). This is like a pledge given to people: 'O people you are safe from me. Your life, your property, your honour is secure with me.'

This sums up the spirit of true religion, the goal of which is spiritual uplift. It is the ultimate state of this spiritual uplift which is referred to in the Qur'an as the "soul at rest" (87:27).

Thus a true and perfect man, from the religious point of view, is one who has reached that level of spiritual development where nothing but peace prevails. When a person has attained that peaceful state, others will receive from him nothing but peace. He may be likened to a flower which can send out only its fragrance to man, it being impossible for it to emit a foul smell.

An incident relating to a saint very aptly illustrates the spirit of religion. The story goes that once a Muslim sufi was travelling along with his disciples. During the journey he encamped near a large grove of trees upon which doves used to perch.

During this halt one of the sufi's disciples aimed at one of the doves, killed it, cooked it and then ate it. Afterwards something strange happened. A flock of doves came to the tree under which the sufi was resting and began hovering over it and making a noise.

The Muslim sufi, communicating with the leader of the birds, asked what was the matter with them and why they were protesting. The leader replied, "We have a complaint to make against you, that is, one of your disciples has killed one of us." Then the Muslim sufi called the disciple in question and asked him about it. He said that he had not done anything wrong, as the birds were their foodstuff. He was hungry, so he killed one for food. He thought that in so doing he had not done anything wrong. The sufi then conveyed this reply to the leader of the doves.

The latter replied: Perhaps you have failed to understand our point. Actually what we are complaining about is that all of you came here in the garb of sufis yet acted as hunters. Had you come here in hunter's garb, we would certainly have remained on the alert. When we saw you in the guise of sufis, we thought that we were safe with you and remained perched on the top of the tree without being properly vigilant.

This anecdote illustrates very well the reality of a true religious person or spiritual person for that matter.

One who has reached the stage of spiritual uplift, and has found the true essence of religion no longer has the will or the capacity to do harm. He gives life not death, to others. He benefits others, doing no injury to anyone. In short, he lives among the people like flowers and not like thorns. He has nothing but love in his heart to bestow upon others.

Now I should like to say a few words about prayer and meditation in Islam. Let me begin with a question from the Qur'an: "When My servants question you about Me, tell them that I am near. I answer the prayer of the supplicant when he calls to Me; therefore, let them answer My call and put their trust in Me, that they may be rightly guided (2:186)."

This verse of the Qur'an tells us that in Islam there is no need for any intermediary to establish contact between God and man. At any time and place man can contact God directly. The only condition is that man should turn to God with sincere devotion.

Islam believes in a personal God. God is an alive being, fully aware of His servants. He hears and sees. That being so, man must call God in all personal matters. Whenever he calls God with a sincere heart, he will find Him close by.

Meditation in Islam aims at bringing man closer to God. When man worships God, when he remembers

Him, when his heart is turned towards Him in full concentration, when he makes a request or a plea, then he establishes a rapport with his Maker. In the words of the Hadith, at that particular moment he comes to whisper with his Lord. He has the tangible feeling that he is pouring his heart out to God and that God in turn is answering his call.

When this communion is established between God and man, man can feel himself becoming imbued with a special kind of peace. His eyes are moist with tears. He starts receiving inspiration from God. It is in moments such as these that man can rest assured of his prayers being granted by God.

According to a *hadith* the Prophet Muhammad said the highest form of worship is to pray as if you were seeing God. We learn from this *hadith* the true sign of a superior form of worship. The true sign is for man to sense the presence of God during worship, and feel that he has come close to God. That is when he can experience the refreshing, cooling effect of God's love and blessings for man. It is this feeling of closeness to God which is the highest form of spiritual experience.

53

Spirituality

What is spirituality? Spirituality — *rabbaniah* — means 'Giving in to God.' The spiritually inclined so elevate themselves in their thinking that they begin to live on a higher divine plane.

They remain undisturbed in the face of provocation, their mental balance is not upset by unpleasant experiences, and the distasteful behaviour of others does not arouse any feelings of anger or revenge in them. Living strictly by their principles, their mental level becomes so high that the status cast by others cannot reach them. In *rabbaniah* they find such sublimity that all else pales into insignificance. *Rabbaniah* in itself is such a great virtue that the seeker after divine bliss need quest no further.

On the other hand, those who have no such spiritual inclinations allow themselves to be constantly influenced by their immediate surroundings and thus unhappily embroiled in human strife. They cannot, like spiritual people, smile when abused. Nor, in countless situations, can they adopt the attitude of 'forgive and forget.' They reach such a low ebb mentally and emotionally, that, spiritually, they become incapable of making progress.

Life's experiences for both the spiritual and the non-spiritual are like the grasping of a rosebush. On each branch are beautifully shaped and coloured blossoms whose scent refreshes from afar the weary in body and spirit. But also on each branch are the inevitable thorns. The spiritual individual will carefully avoid the thorns in order to take possession of the blossom, or if by accident, his hands are pricked by the thorns, he dismisses it as a trivial matter. But the unspiritual person, in his unseemly ways will rudely grasp both thorns and flowers, and will recoil in anger and dismay, baulked of his prize, and burning with resentment.

Where spirituality makes the best of life's experiences — although there is no rose without a thorn — the lack of spirituality makes the worst of them. Where spirituality implies elevation of the soul, the lack of it implies the baser instincts of jealousy, greed, selfishness and exploitativeness.

It will only be when great numbers of the spiritually inclined come together that a society will be formed which shines like the sun and flourishes like lush green gardens.

54

Tawheed

*F*undamental to the religious structure of Islam is the concept of *tawheed*, or monotheism. As the seed is to tree, so is *tawheed* to Islam. Just as the tree is a wonderfully developed extension of the seed, so is the religious system of Islam a multi-facetted expression of a single basic concept. For monotheism in Islam does not mean simply belief in one God, but in God's oneness in all respects. No one shares in this oneness of God.

Anthropologists would have us believe that the concept of God in religion began with polytheism; that polytheism gradually developed with monotheism. That is, the concept of *tawheed* was an evolutionary feature of religion which emerged at a later stage. But, according to Islamic belief, the concept of *tawheed* has existed since the beginning of human life on this earth. The first man—Adam—was the first messenger of God.

It was this first messenger who taught human beings the religion of *tawheed*.

It was in later generations that this religious system began to change. This happened principally because people began to make the assumption that divinity was inherent in natural phenomena. They wondered at the loftiness of the mountains, the unceasing flow of the rivers, and the extraordinary brilliance of the sun and moon, and took it that things possessed of such awesome attributes must necessarily share in God's divinity. Men gifted with special talents likewise came to be included in the category of the divine; they were supposed to be incarnations of God Himself. It was in this manner that the concept of polytheism crept into the religious system.

In consonance with the view that human religions began with *tawheed*—with polytheism as a later development—the basic mission of all the Prophets who made their appearance at intervals in this world was to lead people away from the worship of many gods and back to the worship of the One God. In other words, to turn them away from the adulation of creatures and towards reverence for the Creator.

As a proof of the Creator's existence, the Qur'an advances the very fact of the existence of the universe. All studies of the universe show that it cannot be *sui genesis*: some other agent is essential for the universe to have come into existence. This means that the choice for us is not between a universe with God, or a universe without God. It is rather between a universe with God, or no universe at all. Since a non-existent universe is utterly inconceivable we are forced to accept the option of a universe with God—a necessary condition also for the existence of human beings.

God created man and settled him on the earth. After installing him here, He has kept an unceasing watch over him. Life and death are equally in His hands. Whatever man gains or loses, it is all a matter of the will of God. As the Qur'an expresses it: "God; there is no God but He—the Living, the Eternal One. Neither slumber nor sleep overtakes Him. His is what the heavens and the earth contain. Who can intercede with Him, unless by His leave? He is congnizant of men's affairs, now and in the future. Men can grasp only that part of His Knowledge which He wills. His throne is as vast as the heavens and the earth, and the preservation of both does not weary Him. He is the Exalted, the Immense One." (2:255)

While *tawheed* means the oneness of God, it must be stressed that this concept differs radically from pantheistic or animist notions that all the forms of existence are diverse manifestations of one and the same reality. On the contrary, the oneness of God as defined in Islam means that there is only one Being of the nature of God. All other things of the universe, be they physical or non-physical, are the creations of this One God: they are in no respect constituents of, or partners in the divine godhead.

However, in Islamic theology, *tawheed* does have two aspects to it: *tawheed fi az-Zat* and *tawheed fi as-Sifat*, that is, oneness of being and oneness of attributes. This means that in addition to the fact of there being only one Being who enjoys the status of divinity and possesses divine powers, there is also the fact that no-one else can have a share in, or lay claim to God's attributes. These include the power of creating and sustaining the universe with all its countless bodies in motion, of sustaining and nourishing our world, in short, of governing all the happenings in the heavens and on earth; all of these are directly managed by God. No representative or deputy of God has any power—either independent or delegated—over the events of the universe: "He throws the veil of night over the day. Swiftly they follow one another. It was He who created the sun, the moon and the stars and made them subservient to His will. His is the creation, His the command. Blessed be God, the Lord of all creatures." (7:54)

The divisibility of the divine attributes is totally alien

to Islam. Just as God is alone in His being, so is He alone in His attributes. In recognition of His uniqueness, the Qur'an opens with the following invocation: "Praise be to God, Lord of the universe, the Compassionate, the Merciful, Sovereign of the Day of Judgement. You alone we worship, and to You alone we turn for help. Guide us to the straight path, the path of those whom You have favoured, not of those who have incurred Your wrath, nor of those who have gone astray." (1:1-7)

Thanksgiving

Thanksgiving for man is to acknowledge the blessings of God. This acknowledgement first arises in the heart then, taking the form of words, it comes to the lips of the grateful person.

From birth, man has been superbly endowed in body and mind by his Creator. All his requirements have been amply catered for, every object in the heavens and on earth having been pressed into his service. All the things necessary for his leading a good life on earth and the building of a civilization have been provided in abundance.

Man experiences these blessings at every moment. It is, therefore, incumbent on man to thank God for His blessings at all times. His heart should be eternally brimming with gratitude for these divine blessings.

Thanksgiving is the most comprehensive term of worship: gratefulness is the essence of the godly life. The best expression of that gratefulness is the expenditure of time and money in the way of God. It is God, after all who has given man the reason to worship Him and the means to do so.

56

Tolerance

*T*olerance is a noble humanitarian and Islamic virtue. Its practice means making concessions to others. Intolerance, on the other hand, means showing a self-centered unconcern for the needs of others. Tolerance is a worthy, humane virtue, which has been described in different terms in the shariah: for instance, gentle behaviour, showing concern for others, being soft-hearted, being compassionate.

When true God-worship and religiosity is born within a person, he reaches above all those evils which emanate from selfishness. Instead of living within the confines of the self, he begins to live in the world of reality. The truly pious person begins to look upon people with love and compassion. He does not expect anything from anyone, that is why even when others differ from him or do not behave well towards him, he continues nevertheless to make concessions to them, and continues to be tolerant towards them.

Tolerance implies unswerving respect for others, whether in agreement or disagreement with them. The tolerant man will always consider the case of others sympathetically, be they relatives or friends, and irrespective of the treatment he is given by them, be it of a positive or a negative nature.

Tolerance means, in essence, to give consideration to others. In social life, friction between people does occur in every society, differences arising from religion, culture, tradition and personal tastes persist. In such a situation the superior cause of action is to adopt the ways of concession and large-heartedness without any compromise of principle.

That is to say that the pious man should be a man of principle as far as he himself is concerned, but should be tolerant towards others. He should judge himself in the light of the ideal but in the matter of his fellow men he should show tolerance and broad-mindedness. This being inseparable from human gentility and nobility, Islam aims to produce this fine human quality of gentlemanliness by preaching tolerance.

57

Trial

Man is free in this world. God has not placed any curbs on him. But this freedom is for the purpose of putting man to the test, and is not meant to encourage him to lead a life of permissiveness, like the animals and then just pass away one day. Rather its purpose is that man should lead a morally upright life *of his own free will*, thus demonstrating that he is of the highest moral character.

One who conducts himself in this matter should be reckoned as God's special servant who, without any apparent compulsion, chose to be a man of principle; who, without being subjected to any external force, did of his own free will, what his Lord would have desired. This liberty accorded to man gives him the opportunity to gain credit for being the most superior of all God's creatures.

All the things in this world are God's subjects. The

stars and satellites rotate in space entirely at their Lord's bidding. Trees, rivers, mountains, and all other such natural phenomena are functioning according to the unchangeable ways of God laid down by Him in advance. Similarly, the animals follow exactly those instincts instilled in their species as a matter of Divine Will. Man is the only creature who has been given, exceptionally, the gift of power and freedom.

This freedom has opened doors of two kinds for man, one leading to success and the other to failure. If, on receiving freedom an individual becomes arrogant and insolent, it will mean that he has failed to pass the test.

But if on the other hand, he remains modest and humble, bowing to his Lord's will on all occasions, he will have made the right use of his God-given freedom: he will, without any compulsion, have bound himself by divine principles. One who chooses this course will succeed in the test of freedom. He will be handsomely rewarded by God as no other creature. Held to be the chosen servant of God, he will remain in an everlasting state of blissfulness and blessedness.

58

Wealth

Wealth is one of life's necessities. But it is not life's goal. If wealth is necessary to fulfill life's material requirements, then it must be acquired as the mainstay of human existence. But if wealth is projected as life's goal and its ever-increasing acquisition is considered the most important task, then it can become a source of great misery which will destroy its seekers not only in this world but also in the Hereafter.

Man has to live in this world for a certain period of time. For this, he requires some material facilities which may serve as a support in his life. The majority of these things must be purchased with money. So it is essential for everyone to provide himself with the means to do so. In this respect wealth is a precious asset for all of us.

But perhaps a more important acquisition is that of knowledge. Without knowledge man cannot strive for spiritual progress; he cannot play a positive role in the construction of humanity. He has to acquire knowledge so that he may live in society as a useful and beneficial part of it.

This indeed is a much more worthy goal than the simple acquisition of wealth. But the attainment of this goal is possible only when man devotes the greater part of his energies towards reaching it. The activities of earning money have to be kept within a certain limit and only then will he find time to attain this nobler goal.

Money may fulfill the physical or material needs of man. But it is not sufficient to fulfill his spiritual and intellectual needs. One who makes the acquisition of wealth his life's goal, will of course, continue to receive bodily nourishment, but his soul will all the while have been starving. The intellectual part of his mind, remaining continuously in an under-nourished state, will finally cease to exist.

That is why wealth is called *fitna* (source of trial, that is, it is given to man as a test). The proper use of money leads man to all kind of progress, whereas the wrong use of it casts man headlong into the pit of destruction.

Without Prejudice

During the lifetime of the Prophet of Islam many of his fellow men opposed Islam and engaged in plotting against Islam and Muslims. The Qur'an has mentioned this at several places. But the counter strategy advocated by the Qur'an was not to unearth their plots and launch movements to defeat them, or even finally to wage war against them. On the contrary, the Prophet and his companions were enjoined to place their trust in God alone.

That is to say, ignoring the plots and antagonism, trusting only in God and rising above circumstances, they were to continue all activities which were of a positive nature.

This was an extremely important injunction. By giving this guidance, God set them on a course of positive thinking, which left no room for negative thinking. In short, this Quranic teaching encouraged the early Muslims to live in a self-sufficient way, free of baneful influence of their opponents.

If you have this obsession that others are plotting against you, and that everyone has turned your enemy, it will result in your starting to suspect everyone, to the extent that even if a member of your own community underscores the importance of tolerance and avoidance, you will take it in a negative light and dub him an agent of the enemy. In this way, you will weaken yourselves by turning your own people away from you.

One harmful aspect of such negative obsession is that one loses all objectivity in thinking. One's entire outlook becomes partisan and prejudiced. One is unable to see reality as it is. One becomes like the man who can see only the thorns in a garden of roses or the colour-blind person to whom a garden blossoming with flowers will appear in melancholy shades of grey.

Zakat
(Almsgiving)

By zakat is meant that fixed amount which is subtracted at the end of each year by affluent people. In this way the remaining wealth is purified. By one part of it being given to the cause of God, the rest is rendered lawfully usable for the almsgiver.

Deducting zakat from one's earning is a material acknowledgement of the fact that the actual giver is God. Since the giver is God, the recipient is duty bound to spend it in His cause.

The law of zakat is to take from those who have wealth and give it away to those who do not. This rotation of wealth is a way to balance social inequality. In this way the wealthy are reminded of what is due from them to those who are less well-favoured in life or who are totally destitute.

Zakat is an important part of the Islamic code of ethics. On the one hand, zakat purifies the giver of feelings like miserliness and selfishness, and generates the spirit of generosity and humanitarianism.

On the other hand, the receiver also benefits in the sense that he begins to consider others as his brothers and well-wishers. Thus his heart is not corroded with feelings of jealousy or revenge towards them. Instead, feelings of love and respect are born within him for them.

Since this *zakat* is given for the cause of God, its most important value is that of an act of worship. True, it is distributed among the people, but in its essence it becomes a means of linking the giver with God, of bringing man closer to God.

Zakat in spirit is an act of worship, while in its external form it is the carrying out an act of social service.

Living Islam

By Ruqaiyyah Waris Maqsood

This book examines the social aspects of Islam, clearly outlining the aims and duties of every Muslim in respect of vital issues in Islamic life and conduct. The subjects dealt with include human rights, the sanctity of life, women's rights, the duties of the Muslim in the workplace, the family, sexual relationships, alcohol, drugs, crime and punishment, 'green' issues, and the true meaning of jihad. Reference is made in each chapter to the relevant passages of the Qur'an and Hadith.

The aim of the book is to show how Muslims strive to bring God-consciousness (taqwa) into every area of their daily lives, from the important and profound to mundane and simple tasks; and how, in this devotion and urge to serve, striving for the pleasure of their Lord, they find fulfilment and happiness.

ISBN 81-85063-27-3 Page 310

Muslim Prayer Encyclopaedia

By Ruqaiyyah Waris Maqsood

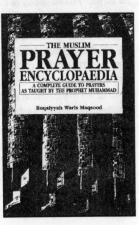

An indispensable guide to the content and practice of Muslim prayer, based on a comprehensive study of all the authentic Hadith of the Prophet Muhammad as presented in the collections of Bukhari, Abu Dawud and Muslim.

ISBN 81-85063-29-X Page 328

The Essential Arabic
A Learner's Practical Guide
By Rafi'el-Imad Faynan

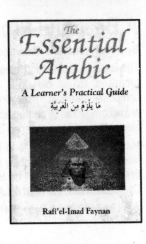

This practical guide to modern Arabic is presented in a very simple and easy-to-grasp style. Unique in its approach, it explains the language by analyzing sample sentences in the kind of crystal clear manner which leaves a lasting impression on the reader's mind. The step-by-step approach of this easy-to-use guide will be found useful not only for beginners, but also for more advanced students. It can also be a handy tool for teachers of the language. One is finally left wondering how the hitherto dreaded learning of Arabic could have been made so delightfully simple...

ISBN 81-85063-26-5 Pages 184

Soul of the Qur'an

By Saniyasnain Khan

Lucid in style and rich in spiritual wisdom, The Soul of the Qur'an is a unique collection of prayers distilled from the Sacred Book. Its one hundred and fifty-four passages, with their exquisite beauty, majestic prose and breadth of vision have been judiciously selected to inspire and uplift the soul.

ISBN 81-85063-13-3, Page 160

Muslim Marriage Guide

By Ruqaiyyah Waris Maqsood

Islam teaches that marriage is 'half of religion'. Because it fulfils so many basic needs of individuals and of society, it is the cornerstone upon which the whole Muslim life is built.

Modern life brings strains and pressures which can upset even the most compatible relationship. This means that nowadays, to protect the spirit of cooperation and happiness which is the sign of the true Islamic marriage, careful thought needs to be given to the mechanisms which help husband and wife to live together and respect each other's rights.

This highly-readable book takes the reader through the relevant passages in the Quran and Hadith, and goes on to discuss the main social and emotional problems that can afflict relationships, suggesting many practical ways in which these can be resolved.

ISBN 81-85063-25-7 Page 192

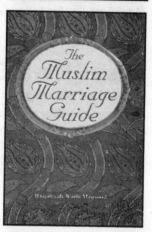

A Beautiful Promises of Allah

By Ruqaiyyah Waris Maqsood

This is a unique collection, gleaned from the Qur'an, of all the promises, full of blessings and grace, and boundless compassionate love, made directly to us by Allah. The texts are accompanied by photographs of natural beauty and holy places that add to our sense of thankfulness and wonder.

May those who accept and believe in the promises be blessed with an uprush of joy and overwhelming gratitude, drawing them closer in love to the Creator, the Compassionate, the Merciful Allah.

ISBN 81-85063-24-0 Page 194

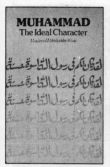

MUHAMMAD
The Ideal Character
Maulana Wahiduddin Khan

Uniform Civil Code
A Critical Study
Maulana Wahiduddin Khan

ISLAM
The Voice of
Human Nature
Maulana Wahiduddin Khan

Polygamy
and
Islam

Tabligh Movement

Maulana Wahiduddin Khan

ISLAM
AS IT IS
Maulana Wahiduddin Khan

Concerning Divorce

Maulana Wahiduddin Khan

THE INTRODUCTION TO ISLAM SERIES **1**

THE WAY TO FIND GOD
Maulana Wahiduddin Khan

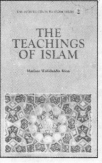

THE INTRODUCTION TO ISLAM SERIES **2**

THE TEACHINGS OF ISLAM
Maulana Wahiduddin Khan

THE INTRODUCTION TO ISLAM SERIES **3**

THE GOOD LIFE
Maulana Wahiduddin Khan

THE INTRODUCTION TO ISLAM SERIES **4**

THE GARDEN OF PARADISE
Maulana Wahiduddin Khan

THE INTRODUCTION TO ISLAM SERIES **5**

THE FIRE OF HELL
Maulana Wahiduddin Khan

रास्ते बन्द नहीं

मौलाना वहीदुद्दीन खान

पैग़म्बरे-इस्लाम एक आदर्श चरित्र

मौलाना वहीदुद्दीन खान

सद्भावी प्रकाशन, नई दिल्ली

उज्जवल भविष्य

मौलाना वहीदुद्दीन खान

पवित्र जीवन

मौलाना वहीदुद्दीन खान

MUHAMMAD
A PROPHET FOR ALL HUMANITY

MAULANA WAHIDUDDIN KHAN

The Wonderful
Universe of
ALLAH

INSPIRING THOUGHTS FROM
THE QUR'AN ON NATURE

COMPILED BY SANIYASNAIN KHAN

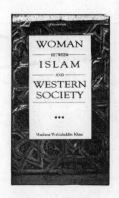

WOMAN
BETWEEN
ISLAM
AND
WESTERN
SOCIETY

•••

Maulana Wahiduddin Khan

QURANIC WISDOM FOR MODERN LIVING

PRESENTING
THE QUR'ĀN

A BRIEF INTRODUCTION TO ALL THE
114 CHAPTERS OF THE QUR'ĀN

SANIYASNAIN KHAN

RELIGION
and
SCIENCE

Maulana Wahiduddin Khan

The
Beautiful
Promises of
Allah

COMPILED BY
RAJSWI WARIS MAQSOOD

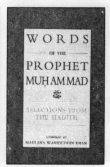

WORDS
OF THE
PROPHET
MUHAMMAD

SELECTIONS FROM
THE HADITH

COMPILED BY
MAULANA WAHIDUDDIN KHAN

THE LIFE OF THE PROPHET
MUHAMMAD

MUHAMMAD MARMADUKE PICKTHALL

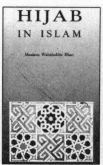

HIJAB
IN ISLAM

Maulana Wahiduddin Khan

The Beautiful
Commands of
ALLAH

COMPILED BY
RAQHSHI WARIS MAQSOOD

WOMAN
IN ISLAMIC SHARI'AH

Maulana Wahiduddin Khan

INDIAN
MUSLIMS

The Need For A
Positive Outlook

MAULANA WAHIDUDDIN KHAN

The
Sayings
of
Muhammad

COMPILED BY
Sir Abdullah Suhrawardy

WITH A FOREWORD BY
Mahatma Gandhi

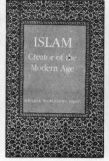

ISLAM
Creator of the
Modern Age

MAULANA WAHIDUDDIN KHAN

QURANIC WISDOM FOR MODERN LIVING

A TREASURY OF
THE QUR'ĀN

PART 1: THE GOD-IDEA

COMPILED BY
MAULANA WAHIDUDDIN KHAN